THE NEW YORK PUBLIC LIBRARY AMAZING NATIVE AMERICAN HISTORY
A Book of Answers for Kids

Liz Sonneborn

A Stonesong Press Book

John Wiley & Sons, Inc.
New York • Chichester • Weinheim • Brisbane • Singapore • Toronto

This book is printed on acid-free paper. ⊗

Copyright ©1999 by The New York Public Library and The Stonesong Press, Inc.
All rights reserved.
Published by John Wiley & Sons, Inc.

Published simultaneously in Canada.

Library of Congress Cataloging-in-Publication Data

Sonneborn, Liz.
    The New York Public Library amazing Native American history: a book of answers
for kids / Liz Sonneborn.
        p.   cm.
    Includes bibliographical references.
    Summary: Questions and answers present information on the history and culture of
various Native American tribes.
    ISBN 0-471-33204-6 (pbk.: acid-free paper)
    1. Indians of North America—History Juvenile literature.
2. Indians of North America—Social life and customs Juvenile literature. [1. Indians of
North America Miscellanea. 2. Questions and answers.] I. Title.
E77.4.S62   1999   99-22916
970.004—dc21

Printed in the United States of America

10 9 8 7 6 5 4 3

CONTENTS

Introduction 1

A Note on the Use of Names 3

THE FIRST AMERICAN INDIANS 5

AMERICAN INDIANS OF MESOAMERICA 17

AMERICAN INDIANS OF THE NORTHEAST 29

AMERICAN INDIANS OF THE SOUTHEAST 51

AMERICAN INDIANS OF THE PLAINS 65

AMERICAN INDIANS OF THE SOUTHWEST 83

AMERICAN INDIANS OF CALIFORNIA 97

AMERICAN INDIANS OF THE NORTHWEST 109

NATIVES OF THE SUBARCTIC AND ARCTIC 125

NATIVES AMERICANS TODAY 139

Glossary 153

Selected Bibliography 156

The New York Public Library's Recommended Reading List 158

Index 160

INTRODUCTION

Why did the Moundbuilders build mounds? Who fought in the French and Indian War? What was the Trail of Tears? Who was Sitting Bull? What is a pow-wow?

These are just a few of the questions you might have about the natives of North America, their history, and their culture. *The New York Public Library Amazing Native American History: A Book of Answers for Kids* answers these and hundreds more. It will introduce you to some of the most important and exciting people, customs, and events that shaped the world of the first Americans. However, it only touches on the huge amount of fascinating facts about Native Americans. To learn more, a good place to look is the New York Public Library, or your own local library.

While reading this book, keep in mind that Indians were never just one people. Before non-Indians came to North America, it was the home of as many as 18 million Indians who belonged to at least three hundred separate tribes. A book this length can't describe every tribe, so for convenience, it covers tribes by region, since Indians living in the same area often had similar ways of life. Whenever possible, though, it highlights the special beliefs, customs, and values that made individual tribes unique.

Much of this book discusses how Indians used to live, but this does not mean they are only people of the past. Native Americans continue to live and thrive throughout North America. In the United States alone, there are more than two million, and this number is growing. In this book's last chapter, you can find information about the Native Americans of today and about the challenges they stand to face in the future.

A Note on the Use of Names

The natives of North America are known by many names. The word Indian was first used after Christopher Columbus and his men sailed to North America in 1492. They thought they had reached the Indies—a term then used to describe parts of Asia—so they called the people they met there Indians. In the late 1960s and early 1970s, many native people spoke out against being called Indians, a term they found inaccurate and insulting. They began referring to themselves as "Native Americans" instead. Today, native people use both terms. In this book, people of Indian ancestry in the past are called "Indians" or "American Indians"; those living now are referred to as "Native Americans." A common Canadian term "Natives" is used to describe that country's native peoples, which include Indians, the Inuit, and the Métis (see the glossary for an explanation of these terms).

Where did the first Indians come from? ◆ How did
the earliest Indians live? ◆ Why did these hunters
move deeper into North America? ◆ What a culture?
When did Indians start to farm? ◆ What were the
first major Indian cultures in the Southwest? ◆ What
was Casa Grande? ◆ What happened to the Mohokam
and Mogollon? ◆ Who were the Anasazi? ◆ What was
Chaco Canyon? ◆ Who were the Cliff Dwellers? ◆ What
happened to the Anasazi? ◆ What was Chaco Canyon?
◆ Who were the Cliff Dwellers? ◆ What happened to
the Anasazi? ◆ Who were the Mound Builders? ◆ How

THE FIRST AMERICAN INDIANS

How do we know about the first American Indians?

One source of information is the work of archaeologists and anthropologists (scholars who study human societies). Archaeologists digging in areas where the first North Americans lived have found bones, tools, and other things the Indians left behind. By examining these objects, archaeologists and anthropologists have been able to piece together a picture of how ancient people used to live. An arrowhead, for instance, might suggest that the people who made it were hunters, or that they had to battle other people to protect their territory.

In addition, some of these ancient humans themselves recorded what animals they hunted, what gods they worshiped, or other information about their lives in drawings and paintings made on cave walls and rock faces. Modern Native Americans also provide clues about their ancestors in ancient stories that have been passed along by word-of-mouth. These stories tell of migrations, battles, and climate changes that their ancestors may have experienced.

Where did the first Indians come from?

Scientists believe that the first Indians came from Asia about 12,000 to 60,000 years ago, when the earth experienced a series of ice ages. With each, much of the earth's waters froze, and in some places the land underneath was exposed. One such area was the Bering Strait. Now a strip of water between Siberia (a region in Russia) and Alaska, the Bering Strait was dry land during the ice ages. Possibly following great herds of animals, ancient Asians walked over this land bridge into North America, becoming the first humans on the continent.

Some Native Americans have another theory about how their ancestors came to live in North America. These ideas are contained in each tribe's creation story—the ancient legend that tells how the tribe was brought into being. The creation story of most tribes says that the first human beings were created in the tribe's homeland. Many Native Americans, therefore, believe that their ancestors did not come from Asia but instead that they have always lived in their traditional lands.

How did the earliest Indians live?

The first Indians in North America were hunters who roamed in small bands following their prey. North America then was the home of many huge beasts, including elephant-like mastodons, great woolly mammoths, and saber-toothed tigers. Humans became adept at chipping stones to make razor-sharp spear points and arrow points that could penetrate the rough hides of these enormous beasts. In addition to providing people with meat, the animals also gave them warm skins to use for clothing and shelter.

The Navajo Emergence

According to the creation story of the Navajo tribe, the Navajo passed through three worlds—the Black World, the Blue-Green World, and the Yellow World—before coming to their southwestern homeland, the Glittering World. Some scholars believe this story confirms their own theory that these early people traveled through the Arctic to central Canada and on to the Rocky Mountain region before settling in the Southwest. In the tribe's story, the Black World recalls the cold, harsh environment of the Arctic; the Blue-Green World resembles the Canadian forests; and the Yellow World features mountains and plains like those on the Rockies' eastern slope.

Archaeologists study a trench that reveals signs of ancient irrigation canals. Studying the structures left by ancient Indians helps us understand their everyday lives.

Why did these hunters move deeper into North America?

As the final ice age came to an end, the weather in North America became warmer. Over many centuries, the descendants of the people who crossed the Bering land bridge traveled farther and farther south, then east. They were always searching for new animals to hunt, in part because the weather changes were causing the mammoths and other large prehistoric animals to die out. By about 11,000 B.C., there were Indians living in all areas of the continent, all surviving by different methods of hunting, fishing, and gathering wild plants. Slowly, as they adapted to their new environments, different groups of people began to develop different cultures.

What is a culture?

A culture is a collection of customs and beliefs that make up a group's way of life. It includes the language the people speak, the beings they worship, the ways they obtain food, the houses they build, the clothing they wear, and the weapons they make to defend themselves and their culture from outsiders. People keep their culture alive by teaching its many elements to each new generation.

When did Indians start to farm?

The first Indian farmers lived in what is now Mexico. In about 5500 B.C., they learned how to grow squash, avocados, and beans. But their greatest achievement was crossing several strains of wild corn to create a new type of corn plant—one that could grow tall and strong in their hot climate.

By about 1500 B.C., knowledge of how to farm corn reached the Indians of the American Southwest. Farming was a boon to these peoples, whose way of life is called the Clovis culture by archaeologists. Their lands were so dry and hot that few animals and plants could live there, so the Indians often had little to eat. By growing their own food, they were no longer in constant danger of starving. Cultivating crops also allowed them to stay in one place because they no longer had to wander in search of wild foods.

What were the first major Indian cultures in the Southwest?

In about A.D. 300, people now known as the Hohokam first established large villages along the Gila and Salt Rivers in what is now southern Arizona. They became successful farmers by digging hundreds of miles of trenches to draw river water to their fields. Their crops included corn, beans, squash, and cotton. Originally, the Hohokam lived in pit houses—simple dwellings made from a wood-and-mud dome built over a pit dug in the ground. By about 1100, they learned to construct larger, sturdier houses out of clay. Many scientists believe the Hohokam were trading partners with people living in what is now Mexico because they shared some customs with these Indians.

At about the same time the Hohokam were building their first villages, the Mogollon founded their own along mountainous streams in present-day southern Arizona and New Mexico. Like the Hohokam, they were farmers who lived first in pit houses and later in clay-walled structures. They learned to weave wild grasses into baskets and cotton yarn into blankets and clothing, which they sometimes decorated with feathers. The Mogollon today are best known for their pottery, which they used to store corn and carry water. Probably the greatest prehistoric Indian potters were the Mogollon of the Mimbres Valley. They painted their pots white, then decorated the surface with red-and-black geometric designs and simple pictures of birds, frogs, and other creatures in their lands.

What was Casa Grande?

Casa Grande (meaning "great house" in Spanish) was built by the Hohokam in about 1325. Located near what is now Florence, Arizona, it was a huge four-story building with a 35-foot tower in the center. The walls were made

The Hohokam traded with Indians living along the Gulf of California for shells. They decorated these treasures by etching animal designs into the shell's surface using the acidic juice of the saguaro cactus.

The Ball Courts of Snaketown

Near present-day Phoenix, Arizona, are the ruins of the village known as Snaketown, where as many as 1,000 Hohokam people lived. Like other Hohokam villages, Snaketown features great shallow oval pits in the ground. Sculptures of ballplayers found at the village suggest the pits were ball courts, where teams came together to play a game similar to soccer.

The Mogollon of the Mimbres Valley often placed a piece of pottery decorated with an animal into a grave. They believed that by breaking a hole in the pot, they could release the painted animal's spirit, who could then guide the dead person to the afterlife.

from bricks of clay called adobe, and the roof was reinforced with great wooden beams that the builders carried from a site more than 50 miles away.

What happened to the Hohokam and Mogollon?

By about 1500, the Hohokam had abandoned their large villages. Although no one knows why for sure, a drought probably made it impossible to grow enough corn to feed large village populations. The Hohokam likely broke into smaller groups who became the ancestors of the Akimel O'odham and Tohono O'odham (also known as the Pima and Papago), two tribes that still live in the Southwest. The Mogollon culture disappeared at about the same time. The Mogollon were probably absorbed into the Anasazi.

Who were the Anasazi?

The Anasazi developed the most advanced early Indian culture in the Southwest. Beginning in about a.d. 100, they lived in the Four Corners area, where the present-day states of Utah, Colorado, Arizona, and New Mexico meet.

Archaeologists call the earliest stage of Anasazi culture the Basket Making period. During this time, the Anasazi learned to weave yucca leaves, bear grass, and other local plants into beautiful and useful baskets. This innovation was a great development in their culture. With baskets, they could easily carry and store crops. Some were so tightly woven that they could even be used to haul water.

An even more important innovation was the creation of adobe houses. At first, these clay houses had only one room. But in time, the Anasazi discovered they could build many rooms next to one another, each sharing a wall with the rooms on either side. The Indians also made these buildings taller by constructing one story on top of each other. Eventually, entire villages lived in huge apartment-like adobe houses.

Anasazi is a Navajo word meaning "ancient ones."

What was Chaco Canyon?

The Anasazi lived in many villages separated from one another by deep canyons. Although the villages were fairly isolated from one another, the Anasazi built a great system of roads so that they could gather together at Chaco Canyon to trade. By about 1050, this massive village was the home of nearly 5,000 people.

Much of the activity at Chaco Canyon revolved around its largest building, Pueblo Bonito, an enormous 800-room housing structure built from more than 1,000,000 adobe bricks. This building was a great feat of architecture. More than 800 years would pass before another structure as large as Pueblo Bonito would be built in what is now the United States.

Pueblo Bonito means "beautiful town" in Spanish. The building was given this name by impressed Spanish explorers who came upon its ruins in the sixteenth century.

Who were the Cliff Dwellers?

The Anasazi were called Cliff Dwellers because some of their largest buildings were built into the walls of cliffs. The most impressive was at Mesa Verde in what is now southwestern Colorado. The great Cliff Palace there was home to about 250 people. One of the first non-Indians to see the ruins of Cliff Palace, F. H. Chapin, compared it to "an immense ruined castle."

It is unclear why the Anasazi started building structures in cliff walls. Perhaps they feared other southwestern Indians who threatened to raid the Anasazi stores of corn. Their cliff dwellings would certainly help shield them from a sneak attack. Another possible reason for building this style of house was that the cliff above provided protection. This roof of rock was a natural shelter from the rain and snow.

What happened to the Anasazi?

In about 1300, the Anasazi suffered a severe drought. Without enough rainfall to grow crops, small groups in

Sheltered beneath a long shelf of overhanging rock, Cliff Palace in Mesa Verde, in present-day Colorado, protected its inhabitants from both invaders and bad weather.

search of food gradually left their large villages. Over time, many resettled along the Rio Grande and its tributaries. The descendants of these people are the Pueblo Indians, who still live in New Mexico and Arizona.

Who were the Mound Builders?

The Mound Builders were the people of three early Indian cultures—the Adena, Hopewell, and Mississippian—that grew up in what is now the central United States from between 500 B.C. and A.D. 1500. They are called Mound Builders because of the most spectacular feature of their villages—enormous structures made by piling earth into huge mounds. Some mounds looked like high hills or pyramids. Others were carefully formed into geometric shapes, such as squares and circles. Still another type, called effigy mounds, were made in the shape of animals. The objects buried in these mounds provide us with much of the information we know about these early people.

How did the Mound Builders live?

The Adena were the first Mound Builders. From about 500 B.C. to A.D. 200, they lived in a large area that covered much of present-day Ohio and Pennsylvania and portions of what are now Indiana, Kentucky, West Virginia, and New York State. They built villages of cone-shaped houses made from poles and bark and obtained most of their food from hunting, fishing, and gathering wild plants. The Adena made simple clay pottery, stone axes and hoes, and beads and jewelry from copper, which they buried in mounds along with their dead.

The next Mound Builders were the Hopewell. Their way of life was similar to the Adena, but their exact relationship to these earlier people is unclear. They may have been the Adena's descendants or may have attacked the Adena and killed them off. The Hopewell culture thrived from about 200 B.C. to A.D. 400. It was centered in southern Ohio but spread over a much larger region that included

One of the first great works of the Mound Builders is the enormous bird-shaped mound at Poverty Point in present-day Louisiana. Built in about 1500 B.C., this mound measures 640 by 710 feet.

present-day Michigan, Wisconsin, Indiana, Illinois, Iowa, Kansas, Pennsylvania, and New York. The Hopewell were great traders who made objects from materials they received from Indians living far from their villages. Their craftspeople made polished stone pipes carved in the shape of animals and animal figures cut from thin sheets of copper and mica (a shiny mineral).

The last Mound Builders were the Mississippians. These people lived from approximately A.D. 800 to 1500, about the time Christopher Columbus first sailed to North America. Built along the Mississippi River and its tributaries, their settlements covered much of what is now the central United States. The Mississippians learned to farm many crops, including corn, beans, and squash. With a steady supply of food, their villages were able to grow larger than those of the Adena and the Hopewell. These large villages probably fought one another; images of warriors are often found in stone sculptures made by the Mississippians. Other objects—such as shells etched with weeping human faces—suggest they had complicated religious beliefs that focused on death and the afterlife.

What was the Great Serpent Mound?

The most famous and well-preserved effigy mound, called the Great Serpent Mound, is located near present-day Peebles, Ohio, where it can still be seen today. Dating from the time of the Adena Culture, the mound is about 5 feet tall, 20 feet across, and nearly a mile long. From the air, it looks like a gigantic uncoiling snake with its mouth open, ready to swallow an egg. The mound may represent the horned serpent, a character in many Indian stories.

Why did the Mound Builders build mounds?

The Adena and Hopewell built mounds as sites to bury their dead. The Mississippians continued this tradition, but they also built a new type of mound—large pyramids with flat tops. The tops of the mounds were places where religious leaders lived and performed rituals. Some later mounds were made as fortifications to keep enemies out.

These stone figurines crafted by a Mississippian artist may have represented the first woman and the first man.

Mound-building itself may also have served a social role by helping people live peacefully with one another. In trading centers such as Poverty Point, where people from many groups came together, working side by side on these great projects may have taught different peoples how to get along.

What was Cahokia?

Before non-Indians arrived in North America, Cahokia was the largest urban center north of present-day Mexico. Located near what is now St. Louis, Missouri, this Mississippian town was at its height in about 1100. It then stretched across more than 200 acres and was the home of nearly 40,000 people. The center also was visited frequently

The Great Monks Mound

Within Cahokia itself, there were 100 or more mounds. Towering over the settlement was the enormous Monks Mound, which rose about 100 feet high. Its base was larger than that of the Great Pyramid of Egypt. It measured 700 feet wide and 1,000 feet long—about the same area covered by 25 football fields.

by traders from far away who canoed the Mississippi River to offer their wares to Cahokia's residents. These traders brought copper from the Great Lakes, shells from the Gulf of Mexico, and glasslike obsidian (volcanic rock) from the Rocky Mountains.

When did the Mound Builders come into contact with non-Indians?

They didn't. By the eighteenth century, when whites began crossing the Appalachians into the Mississippians' lands, their villages were gone. We can only guess at the Mound Builders' fate. Their great settlements may have been laid low by widespread disease or by Indian invaders. Changes in climate may have caused droughts or flooding that destroyed their crops. Or maybe their villages were just too successful, with populations growing so large that they could not be sustained by the resources around them.

Their mounds, however, remained intact. Whites were amazed by these great earthworks. Some, rightly, recognized that these monuments were made by earlier Indian peoples.

Certain whites wrongly assumed that the mounds were built by either Aztec Indians from present-day Mexico or by the lost tribes of Israel told of in the Bible. These whites were so convinced of their superiority over the Indians around them that they could not believe the Indians' ancestors could have created these fantastic structures.

What is Mesoamerica? What is a civilization? Why
did Indian civilizations flourish in Mesoamerica?
How-How well farmed Reflect the lives of Mesoamerican Indians? Who were the Olmec? How did
the Olmec live What objects did Olmec craftspeople
make? What was Teotihuacan? Who were the
Maya? Were the Maya a peaceful people? How do
we know about the Maya What is the Popul Vuh?
What were the Maya's greatest scientific
achievements Who was the Maya calendar What
was a blood sacrifice? What happened to the Maya?
Who were the Toltec? Who were the Aztec?

AMERICAN INDIANS OF MESOAMERICA

What is Mesoamerica?

Mesoamerica is an area that includes central Mexico, Guatemala, Belize, El Salvador, and portions of Honduras and Nicaragua. From about 1200 B.C. to A.D. 1500, the region was home to many of the greatest Indian civilizations, including the Olmec, Maya, Toltec, and Aztec.

What is a civilization?

The word "civilization" is used to describe a society with a complicated political and social structure and distinguished by great achievements in art, architecture, scholarship, and technological know-how.

Why did Indian civilizations flourish in Mesoamerica?

The area was the first place in the Americas where Indians learned to grow their own food. The most important crop was corn, which grew wild in Mesoamerica. These wild corn plants, however, were scrawny, the ears were small, and the corn kernels were tough. It took thousands of years of trial and error before Indians bred a type of corn that could be farmed easily and produce large, healthy ears.

How did farming change the lives of Mesoamerican Indians?

When Indians could grow large amounts of corn, they no longer had to spend every moment trying to find food. They were free to put time into other pursuits. Eventually they developed complicated religious rituals and became skilled craftspeople.

Becoming farmers also meant that Indians had to live in large, permanent settlements to be close to their fields. The larger these villages became, the more the inhabitants looked to political leaders to rule them and religious leaders to guide them. And as populations grew, many laborers could be called upon to make great buildings and monuments.

Who were the Olmec?

The Olmec established the first great civilization in Mesoamerica, which flourished from about 1200 to 400 B.C. It is sometimes called the mother civilization because it had such a great influence on the cultures of later Mesoamerican people, including the Maya and the Aztec. Like the Olmec, these later groups were organized into social classes, were ruled by military and religious leaders, and built large urban centers.

How did the Olmec live?

The Olmec lived primarily along the Gulf Coast east of what is now Mexico City. They built small urban areas—such as those at sites now known as San Lorenzo and La Venta. There, people gathered to trade and attend religious ceremonies. These urban centers featured great public buildings constructed by huge teams of workers. They also built high pyramids with temples at the top, where the Olmec worshiped their many gods.

The Olmec obtained most of their food from farming, but not all of the Olmec people were farmers. Religious leaders performed ceremonies involving human sacrifice. Merchants traded obsidian and mica, which were found hundreds of miles away. Skilled craftspeople used these precious materials to make beautiful objects for the wealthy.

A plaster cast faithfully depicts a colossal head sculpture, one of ten discovered at San Lorenzo, near present-day Mexico City. The Olmec carved these enormous portraits of their rulers out of a hard rock called basalt.

What objects did Olmec craftspeople make?

Olmec artists crafted beautiful ornaments from obsidian and mica. Although they did not have metal tools, they also carved sculptures from granite and jade. Many of these works depicted supernatural beings in the form of alligators, toads, and snakes. The were-jaguar, whose face had features of both a jaguar and a human being, was the most popular supernatural being with artists. Another common type of Olmec figurine seems to depict a bald, chubby baby with its mouth open and twisted as it lets out a loud howl.

What was Teotihuacán?

Teotihuacán was a city that grew up near what is now Mexico City. Between 300 and 900, Teotihuacán was the largest urban area in Mesoamerica. Laid out on an enormous grid, the city featured great open plazas, temples, and palaces.

The Colossal Heads of San Lorenzo

Among the greatest achievements of Olmec art are the great sculptures found at the site of San Lorenzo. Carved from giant blocks of basalt (a volcanic rock), these works depict enormous human heads wearing tight-fitting helmets and probably were meant to be portraits of specific Olmec rulers. Each sculpture measures as tall as five feet and weighs as much as 20 tons.

Amazingly, the basalt used for these colossal heads was not from San Lorenzo. It came from an area more than 60 miles away. Each heavy block was probably pushed to the coast, where it could be loaded onto a raft and floated the rest of the distance.

Rising high above the city was the Pyramid of the Sun. Constructed in about 125, it was as tall as a 20-story building.

Away from the city center were suburbs that spread out over 20 square miles. Some neighborhoods were exclusively for people who practiced a specific craft. Many of these craftspeople made objects out of obsidian, which was treasured by early Mesoamericans. At its height, Teotihuacán was home to perhaps 250,000 people. Centuries after Teotihuacán was abandoned, Aztec visited the ruins. They were so fascinated by its grandeur that they gave the city its name, which means "the place of the gods."

Who were the Maya?

The Maya developed one of the most advanced ancient civilizations in Mesoamerica. At its height from 300 to 800, Maya cities spread over what is now southern Mexico and portions of Belize and Guatemala.

The Maya had much in common with the Olmec. Their skilled farmers grew enough food that many of their people could devote their time to building great cities, performing elaborate religious rituals, creating art, and advancing scientific knowledge.

Were the Maya a peaceful people?

Until recently, scholars thought that the Maya were peaceful. But new research into the records the Maya left behind suggests that they were often at war, often among themselves. At their height, the Maya lived in about 100 separate cities, each with its own ruler. These cities were often trading partners, but just as frequently they were enemies of one another.

How do we know about the Maya?

Unlike most Indian groups, the Maya developed a form of writing to record their history and their religious beliefs. The Maya wrote in hieroglyphs—pictures that symbolized things, ideas, or sounds in their spoken language. They used these symbols to write on stelae (stone tablets) and in codices, books made of long strips of bark folded accordion-style to make separate pages.

What is the *Popul Vuh*?

The *Popul Vuh* is a sacred book that tells the story of how the Maya were created. According to the *Popul Vuh*, the gods first made people from mud. Their bodies were too soft and flexible, so the gods destroyed them. Next, they made humans from wood. Their bodies were too hard and stiff, so the gods sent bats to rip off their heads, jaguars to eat their flesh, and a fiery rain to burn what remained. In their final attempt, the gods used corn to form the Maya. These people pleased the gods because they had souls and minds, so they could worship their creators.

What were the Maya's greatest scientific achievements?

The Maya were amazing astronomers. From observatories atop their great pyramids, they charted the path of Venus and calculated solar and lunar eclipses with an accuracy that would not be matched for many centuries.

They were equally skilled as mathematicians. Maya scholars developed a number system that used only three symbols: a line for five, a dot for one, and a shell for zero. The idea of using a symbol to stand for zero was invented by these ancient mathematicians. They also were the first to use negative numbers.

What was the Maya calendar?

Possibly the Maya's most spectacular achievement was their calendar. Based on their sophisticated astronomical

The largest Maya city, Tikal, spread over 23 square miles, more than three times the size of Rome during the height of the Roman Empire.

research, their calendar was very complicated and very precise. In fact, it was more accurate than the Gregorian calendar we use today.

The Maya calendar was closely tied to their religious beliefs. They thought that an understanding of time was necessary to have a close connection to the gods. They consulted their calendar to schedule religious ceremonies, plan farming activities, and guide nearly every aspect of their lives.

Each day was associated with a specific god. When a baby was born, the child's parents were taken to a religious leader who made predictions about the infant's future and, based on the birth date and time, identified which god would be the baby's patron. To ensure health and happiness, people had to dutifully worship their patron god throughout their lives.

The Maya believed that five days out of the year known as the Uayeb were extremely unlucky. During these days, they fasted to ward off danger.

What was a blood sacrifice?

The Maya performed many rituals and ceremonies to keep their gods happy. Some involved the shedding of human blood. Captives taken in war were sometimes killed to please the gods. But even powerful people, such as rulers and religious leaders, were expected to make blood sacrifices. Commonly, they drew their own blood by piercing their tongue and threading a rope through the hole.

Playing Ball

At their most prosperous, the Maya's cities featured more than 400 ball courts. These playing fields were the site of spirited and often violent games. Like basketball, a team scored when one of its players made a rubber ball fall through a hoop. Like soccer, though, players could not throw the ball with their hands, but instead had to move the ball by bumping it off with their wrists, elbows, or hips.

Unlike modern sports, however, the Maya ball game was often a death match—literally. War captives sometimes were forced to play for their lives. One piece of evidence of how deadly these games could be is a carved stone panel that decorated the ball court at the city of Chichén Itzá. It depicts a victorious player holding the severed head of his opponent.

Gods of the Maya

Itzamna: The lord of the heavens and the god of learning and writing. Itzamna was often depicted in Maya art as a two-headed serpent.

Ix Chel: The wife of Itzamna and the goddess of medicine and childbirth. All other gods were the children of Ix Chel and Itzamna.

Chacs: The gods of rain. Chacs were especially revered by farmers, whose crops would flourish only if they stayed in the Chacs' good graces.

Kinich Ahau: The god of the sun from when it rose to when it set. After setting, the sun was thought to travel into a world of darkness where it was ruled by the Jaguar god.

What happened to the Maya?

In about 900, the Maya civilization began to decline. The reason for this decline is not clear. The Maya may have overfarmed the land, leaving the soil barren. They may also have fallen victim to epidemics or been ruined by constant warfare.

The descendants of the Maya lived on, but with little of their former glory. They were treated brutally by Spanish conquistadores in the sixteenth century and discriminated against by descendants of those Spaniards who settled in the region. Today, Maya people in Mexico and neighboring Guatemala are working to preserve their culture while trying to improve their economic opportunities.

Who were the Toltec?

While the Maya civilization was in decline, the Toltec came to power in what is now central Mexico. United under the leader Mixcoatl, they established a vast empire in the region.

A warlike people, the Toltec not only dominated other groups, they also set about building a great civilization. Led by Mixcoatl's son, Topiltzin, Toltec artists and scholars studied the work of earlier Mesoamerican cultures and adapted them to create their own body of knowledge. Like other Mesoamerican cultures, the Toltec also built large cities. The greatest was their capital of Tula, which extended over three square miles and had a population in the tens of thousands.

The Toltec artists crafted large stone sculptures called chacmools. *Placed by a ruler's throne,* a chacmool *depicted a fallen warrior lying on his back. On the warrior's torso was a vessel used to hold the hearts of human sacrifices.*

The Toltec civilization lasted for only about 200 years. The Toltec lost control over their lands in about 1200, as roving bands of hunters moved into the region. These hunters, now known as the Chichimeca ("people of the dog"), included the ancestors of the Aztec Indians.

Who were the Aztec?

The Aztec created perhaps Mesoamerica's greatest ancient empire. When their ancestors first came to central Mexico, however, they were little more than barbaric hunters. Early on, these people were under the control of more powerful Chichimeca tribes, for whom they sometimes served as warriors in exchange for pay. To escape from the demands of these tribes' leaders, the Aztec retreated to a muddy island in the center of a great lake ringed by mountains, the site of what is now Mexico City. There, they built the city of Tenochtitlán, where they prospered and their population grew.

In the early 1400s, the Aztec were strong enough to rebel against the tribes that dominated them. United under the ruler Itzcóatl, they became the most powerful people in the region by about 1440. The Aztec kings to follow extended their rule by sending out armies to conquer cities throughout what is now central Mexico. In less than a century, the Aztec established a vast empire of about 400 cities and a population of approximately 5,000,000.

What was Tenochtitlán like?

By the sixteenth century, Tenochtitlán had a population of about 400,000, making it the largest Indian city ever built in Mesoamerica. The city was originally established on a small island. As Tenochtitlán grew in size, its inhabitants took over a neighboring island, Tlatelolco, and built bridges to make it accessible to Tenochtitlán. In an even greater engineering feat, they actually increased the size of the land on which Tenochtitlán rested. After anchoring baskets to the shallow bottom of the surrounding lake, they covered them with soil and vegetation to create small new floating islands onto which the city could expand.

Among the largest buildings in the Aztec capital were spectacular temples. The largest honored Huitzilopochtli, the god of war and of the sun, who the Aztec believed chose them to rule their enormous empire. Nearby was a great palace with two stories—one with living quarters for the ruler and his family, the other with offices from which the vast empire could be run. Within the city, there were also schools, ball courts, zoos, and a huge market where food and goods were traded.

What was tribute?

Tribute was food and goods the Aztec ruler demanded from the people he conquered. By collecting tribute, the Aztec Empire financed the splendors of Tenochtitlán and the nobility's lavish way of life. At the empire's height, tribute was collected from 489 cities. Farmers were required to give up a certain percentage of their crop. Craftspeople and traders gave luxury items such as gold, feathers, gems, jade, jaguar skins, and chocolate. Many people resented having to pay tribute, but they were even more angered when Aztec armies raided their cities. These warriors attacked for the

The ruins of Tenochtitlán became the foundation for another great urban center, Mexico City— today the capital of Mexico and that country's largest metropolis.

Artist Ignacio Marquina created this image of the Great Temple of Tenochtitlán by studying descriptions by Spanish conquerors and by looking at surviving Aztec monuments.

The Place of the Cactus

According to the Aztec legend, the god Huitzilopochtli led the Aztec to the place where Tenochtitlán would be built. At the site, they found an eagle seated on a cactus holding a serpent in its beak. This image now appears in the center of the Mexican flag. The legend also lives on in the name Tenochtitlán, which means "place of the cactus" in Nahuatl, the language of the Aztec.

sole purpose of taking captives, who were brought to Tenochtitlán and killed as human sacrifices.

Why did the Aztec perform human sacrifices?

Always in fear of droughts that would dry up their food supply, the Aztec people felt their future was uncertain. They believed that the only way to guarantee their survival was to please the gods they worshiped by offering them human sacrifices. During the dedications of temples and other ceremonies, tens of thousands of captives were probably sacrificed to ensure the empire's well-being.

Who was Quezalcóatl?

Quezalcóatl was an honored god of the Toltec and became an important deity for the Aztec as well. To the Aztec, he was the god of corn and of the arts. According to their legends, Quezalcóatl once had been a man. After angering the gods, the human Quezalcóatl had been exiled from the Aztec world, but he promised one day to return to his people. Aztec artists pictured Quezalcóatl the god as a feathered serpent, but in his human form he was a tall, light-skinned man with long hair and a beard.

Who was Hernando Cortés?

Cortés, a Spanish explorer, arrived at the coast of present-day Mexico in 1519 with an army of about 350 soldiers. Cortés was searching for a great city rumored to be full of riches. As they moved inland, Cortés and his men battled some of the Indians they met, but they were able to persuade many others to join them. Nearly 1,000 natives, tired of paying tribute and supplying human sacrifices, joined up to fight alongside the European strangers against their enemies in the Aztec capital.

As Cortés approached Tenochtitlán, he was met by ambassadors sent by Montezuma, then the Aztec ruler. They gave the Spaniards gifts, and when they arrived in the city, Montezuma himself welcomed them as guests.

Why didn't Montezuma attack Cortés's men?

For the ten years prior to Cortés's arrival, odd happenings had haunted the Aztec. Elders had peculiar and upsetting dreams. Lightning struck a temple honoring the god of fire. The waters of the lake surrounding Tenochtitlán turned rough unexpectedly. Religious leaders feared these were omens of impending disaster.

When Cortés arrived in their lands, many, including Montezuma, were relieved. With his light complexion and dark facial hair, Cortés seemed to be the god Quezalcóatl, as he was described in Aztec legend, who as promised had at last come back to earth. The omens, they reasoned, had foretold Quezalcóatl's return, not the end of the universe as they feared.

Cortés returned Montezuma's hospitality by taking him hostage. As the Spaniard tried to take over the city, the Aztec began to fight Cortés's men. They drove off their enemies, but during the conflict, Montezuma was killed. Even worse, the Spanish were not gone for long. On April 28, 1521, Cortés led 900 Spanish soldiers and thousands of Indian allies in a full-scale assault on Tenochtitlán. The Aztec's arrows, clubs, and lances were no match for the Europeans' swords, guns, and cannons. The great Tenochtitlán was destroyed, shattering the entire Aztec empire.

Did the Spanish kill all of the Aztec?

No. Many Aztec died during the Spanish invasion, and still others were killed in the years that followed by non-Indian diseases introduced to them by the Spanish. Those who survived were subjugated by the strangers in their land. Over time, the Spanish forced their children and their children's children to adopt Spanish ways. But despite the Spaniards' efforts, the Aztec continued to practice their own religious rites and preserve their culture.

The lands of the Aztec are now part of the country of Mexico. To a large extent, their descendants have been absorbed into the general Mexican population. But some elements of the great Aztec empire live on. More than 1,000,000 people continue to speak the Aztec language. Many still make pottery, cloth, and other works of art using ancient techniques. And although most are practicing Christians, some still honor the Aztec gods of old by associating them with Catholic saints.

AMERICAN INDIANS OF THE NORTHEAST

Who were the first tribes in the Northeast?

Before non-Indians arrived in North America, the woodlands of the Northeast were the home of some 50 tribes. Anthropologists group most of these peoples as either Algonquian or Iroquoian. The tribes in each group were distant relatives of one another. They also spoke similar languages and shared many of the same customs and ways.

Where did the Algonquian live?

The northeastern Algonquian were clustered in two areas. One group lived near the Great Lakes in what is now the north-central United States and south-central Canada. The Great Lakes Algonquian tribes included the Ojibwa (also called the Chippewa), the Menominee, and the Potawatomi.

Other Algonquian lived along the coast of the Atlantic Ocean from present-day Nova Scotia, Canada, to North Carolina. Among these groups were the Micmac, the Eastern and Western Abenaki, the Wampanoag, the Narragansett, the Lenape, and the tribes of the Powhatan Confederacy.

Why did the Algonquian settle near water?

The Algonquian sought out spots near the water so that they would always be near fish or other water creatures to eat. Tribes on lakes and rivers invented all types of hooks, spears, and nets to catch fish. Those living on the Atlantic shore also gathered oysters, clams, and shellfish. The Wampanoag of present-day Massachusetts, for instance, often enjoyed dinners of fresh lobster.

Farther north, Micmac hunters, armed with clubs, stalked seals as they searched the coast for whales that had washed ashore. When a whale was found, an entire village might come together to share a meal of whale meat on the beach.

Waterways also served as Algonquian's highways. In watertight canoes, they took fishing expeditions, made trips to visit friends and relatives, and traded with people in other villages.

What was a dugout?

A dugout was a type of canoe used by many Algonquian tribes. To make a dugout, a canoe-maker started by chopping down a cedar or an elm tree and setting the middle of the trunk on fire. Once the trunk was charred and the flame extinguished, the burned wood in the center would be dug out.

Large dugouts could carry as many as 30 people, but they were too heavy and awkward to take through the

The Wild Rice People

Many Great Lakes tribes ate the delicious rice that grew wild in their marshlands. But this food was most important to the Menominee, whose very name meant "wild rice people."

Every year, late in the summer, the Menominee took a fleet of canoes through marshes where rice stalks grew up high above the water. While some paddled, others would grab the stalks, pull them over the boats, and beat them with wooden sticks until husks full of ripe rice seeds fell into the canoes. Back home, they separated the seeds from the husks and dried them in the sun.

Once the work was done, the Menominee could count on feasting all winter long on steaming bowls of boiled rice. Instead of salt, they added maple syrup to flavor their meal.

twists and turns of winding waterways. For this purpose, northern coastal tribes, such as the Narragansett, built their canoes from the bark of the birch tree. Unlike dugouts, these canoes were lightweight and easy to handle in even the narrowest rivers and inlets.

Did the Algonquian farm and hunt?

Most of the Algonquian lived in a region full of rich, well-watered land—ideal for growing crops, such as beans and squash. Corn was especially important to the Algonquian living along the mid- and southern Atlantic Coast. This one crop made up almost half of their diet.

With much of their lands covered by rich forests, clearing fields was hard work. As many as 50 people might work together to burn and clear trees from an area. Men performed most of this labor, but women did all the planting, tending, and harvesting.

Uncleared forests offered the Algonquian still other sources of food. In the woods, women gathered nuts and berries, while men hunted game animals, such as deer, rabbits, and turkeys. The Algonquian also made clothing out

Wild rice was an important food for many Great Lakes tribes. An engraving depicts Ojibwa Indian women harvesting wild rice in a canoe—the best way to get around the marshlands where this rice grew in abundance.

Some Algonquian called strawberries "heartberries" because of their color and shape.

of animal furs and skins and tools from their bones, antlers, and teeth.

What was a wigwam?

Many Algonquian tribes favored the type of house known as a wigwam. It was constructed from a frame of saplings bent to form a dome. Over this frame, wigwam builders tied mats of woven grass or reeds or sheets of tree bark. Wigwams were easy to set up and easy to take down—important features for hunters in the north who followed herds of deer and moose. These portable houses were also useful as campsites for people gathering berries and wild plants. Year after year, a family might set out for the same berry patch when the fruit was ripe for picking. For easy camping, they might leave a wigwam frame by the patch, so they only had to carry the mat or bark walls with them.

What was the Midewiwin?

The most distinguished healers among the Ojibwa tribe were the members of the Grand Medicine Society, or Midewiwin. To enter the society, men and women had to undergo a lengthy initiation, during which they learned about herbal medicines and were trained in the special songs and ceremonies of the Midewiwin. Achieving all four ranks of the Midewiwin could take as long as 20 years. Only those who displayed great bravery and honor were able to reach the highest level. These healers inspired fear as well as respect in their fellow Ojibwa. Through their contact with spirits called manitous, they possessed great power, which they could use as easily for evil as for good.

Where did the Iroquoian live?

The northeastern Iroquoian tribes lived in what is now central and western New York State and southern Ontario, Canada. These lands were sandwiched between the territory of the Great Lakes Algonquian tribes and that of the Algonquian tribes along the northern Atlantic Coast.

Before contact with whites, there were about 12 Iroquoian tribes in the Northeast. These peoples included

the Huron, the Neutral, the Erie, and the tribes of the
Iroquois Confederacy.

*Ojibwa women
made works
of art by biting
decorative shapes
into pieces of
birch bark.*

What was the Iroquois Confederacy?

In about 1400, five great tribes—the Cayuga, Mohawk,
Oneida, Onondaga, and Seneca—banded together to form
the Iroquois Confederacy. (The confederacy was also
called the Iroquois League or the Five Nations.)

A sixth tribe—the Tuscarora—joined the confederacy
in 1722. The Tuscarora were a Iroquoian tribe from what is
now North and South Carolina. They traveled north and
settled near the Oneida after English settlers drove them
from their homeland.

The Iroquois tell stories of a dark time before the confederacy when the different tribes were enmeshed in
blood feuds. When someone was murdered, the victim's
relatives were bound to avenge the death by killing the
murderer or one of the killer's relatives. This practice led
to a cycle of murder and revenge that could last many
years and destroy entire families. Finally, a man named
Hiawatha (sometimes spelled Hayenwathe) got the tribes
to agree to make peace.

Who was Hiawatha?

According to Iroquois legend, Hiawatha was an
Onondaga man who refused to take revenge on those
who murdered his wife and children. He instead looked
for comfort in the words of a prophet the Iroquois now
call the Peacemaker. The Peacemaker instructed Hiawatha
in the Great Law—a set of rules for settling disputes without violence.

Hiawatha traveled through the Iroquois tribes
spreading the Peacemaker's message. The Mohawk,
Cayuga, Oneida, and Seneca agreed to live in peace, but
the Onondaga refused. This tribe was under the influence of a powerful leader named Thadodaho. Hiawatha
soothed Thadodaho's evil nature by combing out the
snakes that grew wildly from his head like hair. Hiawatha
then persuaded Thadodaho to support the confederacy
by making the Onondaga the Keepers of the Central Fire.
Around this fire, the leaders from each tribe were to

In 1855 Henry Wadsworth Longfellow wrote a famous poem titled "The Song of Hiawatha." His Hiawatha, however, was not the great Iroquois leader, but a fictional character based on the legendary Algonquian hero Nanbozho. Longfellow confused the two because he used inaccurate research compiled by non-Indians.

come together every year to confirm their allegiance to one another.

Did the Iroquois fight other Indians?

Although the members of the Iroquois Confederacy pledged not to war with one another, they were often ferocious in battles with other tribes. The Iroquois often fought against neighboring Algonquian and Iroquoian tribes—especially the Huron, whom they considered their greatest enemy.

Successful warriors brought captives taken in battle back to their village. A captive's fate was in the hands of the village's women. Sometimes they ordered that the captive be put to death, often by being tied to a stake and set on fire. At other times, the women chose to adopt the captive as a full member of the tribe. Adopting captives helped keep the number of young men in a village constant, since they could replace men killed in battle.

What was a longhouse?

A longhouse was the traditional Iroquois dwelling. This enormous barn-shaped structure was made from a frame of saplings covered with bark shingles. Several longhouses were built near one another to form small villages.

A longhouse was usually about 18 feet wide but could range from 40 to 200 feet long, depending on how many people lived there. Two holes, one in each of the two narrow sides, served as entrances. Small holes were also left in the roof to let sunlight in and smoke out. The smoke came from small fires set in a long row inside the longhouse. The fires were used to cook food and to heat the house during the winter.

The Grand Council of the Iroquois

The Iroquois Confederacy was governed by the Grand Council, which was composed of 49 men with representatives from every tribe. Each council member was given a title, which was the name of one of the 50 leaders who attended the first council. One name, however, was never assigned—that of the great Hiawatha. By refusing to name a new Hiawatha, the Iroquois honored his special role as a founder of the confederacy.

Several families—sometimes as many as 24—lived together in a single longhouse. Each family had its own living area along the side of the house and shared a fire with people in the living area directly across from them. The people who shared a longhouse were usually close relations who all belonged to the same clan.

Some Algonquian tribes, including the Abenaki and the Lenape, lived in longhouses like the Iroquois.

Who were the Hodenosaunee?

Hodenosaunee, meaning "People of the Longhouse," is the name that the Iroquois traditionally used to refer to themselves. The Iroquois believed that their confederacy was like a longhouse. Just as several families dwelled in harmony side by side in the same longhouse, the Iroquois lived peacefully in adjoining nations within the same realm.

The confederacy-longhouse comparison also gave special names to the Mohawk, Seneca, and Onondaga. Because longhouses had two doors, one at either end, the Mohawk (the easternmost tribe) were called the "Keepers of the Eastern Door," and the Seneca (the westernmost tribe) were known as the "Keepers of the Western Door." And because household fires were set in the center of the longhouse, the Onondaga, who lived in the middle of Iroquois territory, were given the name "Keepers of the Central Fire."

What was a clan?

A clan was a group of relatives who all shared the same ancestor. In each village lived people from several different clans. The clans were named after animals the Iroquois valued—the bear, deer, beaver, turtle, wolf, and hawk. A carved image of one of these animals was often placed above a longhouse entrance to show the clan of the people who lived inside.

Among the Iroquois, children belonged to their mother's clan. A person could only marry someone from a different clan. A boy would live in the longhouse of his mother's clan, but when he got married, he would move into the longhouse where his wife and her family lived.

Who led the clans?

Local problems and disputes were usually settled by village councils. In these councils, each clan was represented by several men. These leaders were chosen by the clan's most prominent women, known as clan mothers. Although these women could not speak in council, they wielded the real power. Before councils were held, clan mothers met and discussed political matters, then explained to their leaders what they should say in the meeting.

Councilmen almost always did as they were told. If they did not, they risked being "dehorned." At a dehorning ceremony, angry clan women stripped a disobedient clan leader of the special headgear (decorated with deer antlers) that councilmen wore. Not only did a dehorned councilman lose his position; he was also humiliated in front of everyone in his village.

Who were the Three Sisters?

Corn, beans, and squash, the foods the Iroquois relied on most were known as the Three Sisters. Like the northeastern Algonquian tribes, the Iroquois had many food sources, including wild plants, game animals, and fish, but their most important source of food was the crops they cultivated.

The Three Sisters were thought to be gifts from Our Mother, a figure in Iroquois legends. After Our Mother died while giving birth to Evil Twin, corn grew from her heart, squash from her stomach, and beans from her fingers. Her other son, Good Twin, taught the Iroquois how to grow these plants, thus ensuring their prosperity and well-being.

What was a False Face?

During some curing rituals, Iroquois medicine men danced while wearing carved wooden masks called False

Snowsnakes

After a heavy winter snow, Seneca men often gathered to play their favorite sport—snowsnakes. A snowsnake was a long wooden pole polished to a slippery finish with beeswax. In the game, the players took turns sliding their "snakes" along a shallow ditch dug into the snow. The winner was the player whose snowsnake traveled the farthest.

Faces. Many of these masks featured deep-set eyes, a crooked nose, and a huge mouth twisted into a grimace.

Healers wore these False Faces to honor Shagodyo-wehgowah. According to the Iroquois' ancient stories, he was a giant who challenged the Creator to a contest to see who had the greater spirit-power. As both sat with their backs to a mountain, the Creator used his power to move it toward them. When Shagodyowehgowah turned to see what the Creator was doing, the mountain smacked into his nose, crushing it onto one side of his face. Defeated, the giant promised the Creator to use his powers to help heal ailing Iroquois if they showed him respect through their rituals.

Because Iroquois women planted and tended the fields, they owned the harvest. If a woman was angry with her husband, she had the right to refuse to give him food from the family's stores.

When did northeastern Indians first meet non-Indians?

In 1497, only five years after Christopher Columbus's voyage to North America, John Cabot, an Italian-born explorer heading an English expedition, sailed to what is now Newfoundland in northeastern Canada. During a second voyage, the next year, he probably came upon Indians of the Beothuk tribe.

Cabot was soon followed to the Northeast by a steady stream of European explorers, fishermen, and traders, who became the first whites encountered by the tribes living along the Atlantic Coast. Most of these visitors came from England, France, and the Netherlands (also called Holland).

Europeans did not try to settle in the Northeast until about 100 years later. The English were the first to attempt to build permanent colonies. They founded Roanoke (1585) in present-day North Carolina, Jamestown (1607) in what is now Virginia, and Plymouth (1620) in present-day Massachusetts. While the colonists became accustomed to their new home, all relied on help from local Indians for their survival.

Was the Lost Colony of Roanoke really lost?

The mystery of Roanoke began in 1590 when colony leader John White, returning from a three-year trip to England for supplies, found the settlement deserted. All of the colonists had seemingly disappeared.

According to some theories, though, the Roanoke colonists were not lost, but found—by Indians. Some

The Iroquois believed that False Faces were living things that had to be fed meals of corn mush to stay alive.

Huron Dream-Guessing

Hundreds of years before psychiatrists began analyzing their patient's dreams, the Huron people believed that nightmares held hidden clues to a person's innermost desires. Once a year, they held a ceremony called Ononharoia (meaning "upsetting the brain") to examine their dreams.

The ceremony began on a winter night. In the cold and dark, everyone troubled with bad dreams ran crazily through the village, stumbling into other families' longhouses and riffling through their possessions. The next day, they returned to these houses and asked the inhabitants to guess what they had dreamed about the night before. Each guesser had to give the dreamers an object, such as a tool or a pot, that their dream showed they secretly wanted. Dreamers went from guesser to guesser until someone gave them the thing they wanted most. With their dream fulfilled, they were then cured of all their bad thoughts.

scholars believe that nearby Indians grew tired of English living on their lands and killed them. Others hold that the colonists, starving and desperate, were saved by Indians who gave them food and shelter in their own villages. The Lumbee of North Carolina believe that their ancestors were the Indians who adopted the colonists into their tribe. The Lumbee say this explains why some tribe members had blue eyes (a non-Indian trait) long before the tribe had regular contact with whites.

Who was Pocahontas?

Born in about 1596, Pocahontas was the favorite daughter of Powhatan, a powerful Indian leader who ruled about 30 tribes in what is now Virginia. When the English built Jamestown on her father's lands, she was probably about 11 years old. Like many of the Powhatan Indians, she took an interest in the English and their unfamiliar ways. At her father's request, Pocahontas also delivered gifts of food to the colonists.

Despite the hospitality of the Powhatan people, the friendly relationship between the Indians and the English quickly broke down. In 1610 Pocahontas stopped visiting their settlement. Three years later, she was kidnapped by the English, who used her as a tool in their negotiations with Powhatan. While living in Jamestown, Pocahontas married John Rolfe, a wealthy colonist and took the Christian name Rebecca. In 1616, Jamestown leaders sent her to England, where they introduced her to powerful people, including the king, while they tried to raise money for the colony. On her trip home, Pocahontas became sick and died at the age of about 21.

Did Pocahontas want to live among the English, as they claimed, or was she being held captive against her will? No one knows for certain.

Did Pocahontas save the life of Captain John Smith?

Probably not. This famous legend was written by John Smith himself, whose stories about his dramatic adventures

This engraving of Pocahontas was based on her appearance when she was in England, where she was known as Rebecca. It is the only likeness of her based on her real appearance, not the artist's imagination.

were usually exaggerated, if not completely made up. According to Smith, who was a Jamestown leader, a group of Powhatan's warriors took him captive in December 1607. They brought him to Powhatan, who forced Smith to kneel before him. Just as Powhatan's men were about to crack his skull with wooden clubs, Powhatan's young daughter Pocahontas ran in, threw her own body over Smith's, and convinced her father to spare his life. Smith was then treated to a great feast and released.

If Smith didn't invent this story altogether, he may have misinterpreted the events. Instead of trying to execute Smith, Powhatan may have been staging a special ceremony his people used to adopt someone into their tribe. During the ceremony, Powhatan's daughter may have just been playing the role of Smith's "savior" as a way of symbolically making the Englishman Powhatan's adopted son.

Did Indians celebrate Thanksgiving with the Pilgrims?

Massasoit, the chief of the Wampanoag, and about 90 of his warriors joined the Pilgrims at Plymouth for a thanksgiving feast in the autumn of 1621. Following Indian tradition, the celebration was held to thank God for a plentiful harvest. The Pilgrims owed their Wampanoag guests a great debt because the Wampanoag had taught them how to farm in their new land. Although the relationship between the Wampanoag and the Pilgrims was sometimes strained, Massasoit encouraged his people to help the English colonists in order to keep the peace.

What was King Philip's War?

King Philip's War was the name the English gave to a series of attacks the Wampanoag and Narragansett Indians made on the Plymouth Colony in 1675. The attacks were led by Metacom, the sachem (leader) of the Wampanoags and son of Massasoit. Unlike his father, Metacom did not trust the English, especially after his brother Wamsutta died following a meeting with Plymouth's leaders. Suspecting that Wamsutta had been poisoned, Metacom, with the support of Wamsutta's powerful widow, Weetamoo, rallied nearby villages to battle the English intruders.

The English nicknamed Metacom "King Philip" after the ancient king Philip of Macedon. Like Philip, Metacom proved to be a great military leader. The English, however, had many more guns, and the Indians were quickly overpowered. The war came to an end in August 1676, when the English killed Metacom and placed his severed head on a high post as a grim threat to other would-be Indian rebels.

What was the fur trade?

Beginning in the late 1500s, traders from France, England, and the Netherlands flocked to North America to trade with Indians for animal furs. Europeans wanted furs to make warm winter clothing. The demand was so great that European traders could make a fortune by filling their ships with furs and reselling them in Europe.

Northeastern Indian hunters sometimes traded furs for trinkets such as glass beads and mirrors. Indians were fascinated by these items, which they had never seen before they had contact with whites. Most often, though, Indians wanted practical goods such as metal tools and cloth. These items, manufactured in Europe, were also new to Indians. They found that metal axes, knives, and pots lasted far longer than similar items they made themselves from bone, stone, and clay. Likewise, they discovered that cloth was easier to sew and often more comfortable to wear than animal skins.

How did the fur trade affect northeastern Indians?

Some of the trade goods Indians received from Europeans made their work easier and their lives more comfortable. But the fur trade's bad effects far outweighed the good. As Indians became involved in the fur trade, their way of life, if not their lives themselves, were often threatened.

One tragic effect of the fur trade was exposure to European diseases. Through contact with traders, Indians caught smallpox, measles, and other diseases that were new to North America. Because Indians had no natural immunities to them, these foreign diseases killed thousands of northeastern Indians.

In 1682, a colonist named Mary Rowlandson published an account of her 13 weeks as a Wampanoag captive during King Philip's War. Next to the Bible, it was the best-selling book in colonial America.

The Fashionable Beaver

When the fur trade began, European traders most wanted lush pelts of mink, sable, black fox, and ermine, which were used to trim expensive coats worn by the wealthy. By about 1600, though, the fur most in demand was that of the beaver, an animal nearly extinct in Europe. Felt hats were then a very popular European fashion. Durable and naturally water repellent, the best felt was made from the beaver's soft underfur.

Because of the fur trade, Indian men also began spending more time hunting than ever before. In addition to wiping out entire animal populations, overhunting gave Indians far less time to make the tools, utensils, and clothing they needed. They instead began to rely on European traders for these items.

This dependence on European goods gave Europeans control over Indian peoples. For instance, the French might demand that their Indian trading partners help fight their British competitors. The Indians had to do as the French asked, or the French might cut off their supply of goods. This type of warfare often pitted Indians allied to one group of Europeans against Indians allied to another.

What were the Beaver Wars?

In 1643 the powerful Iroquois tribes became the allies of the Dutch (the people of the Netherlands). They promised to give the Dutch furs in exchange for guns—an arrangement that spelled doom for many of the Iroquois' enemies. In the next decade, they would battle the Petun, the Neutral, and the Erie, but their most brutal war was against the small Huron tribe. The Iroquois were jealous of the Huron's success as middlemen in the fur trade. The Huron had become rich by trading corn to northern tribes for thick beaver pelts, which the Huron then traded to their French allies for European goods.

In the spring of 1649, Mohawk and Seneca warriors attacked Huron villages with a viciousness rarely seen before in Indian warfare. They killed many of the Huron and drove the rest out of their lands. Some Huron escaped

Indian traders called Europeans "cloth men," "knife men," or "iron men," depending on the goods they offered.

to what is now Quebec, Canada. Others, later called the Wyandot, fled west to lands in present-day Michigan and Ohio. Still others were adopted by the Iroquois to replace warriors killed in battle. Although these survivors would build new lives in new homelands, the Huron would never live as one tribe again.

What was the Pequot War?

One of the most brutal conflicts in colonial America was the Pequot War (1636–37), during which the English killed hundreds of Pequot Indians—a small tribe in present-day Connecticut. The war nearly destroyed the Pequots. The few survivors tried to keep the tribe alive, but as time passed their population dwindled. By 1930, the two branches of the tribe—the Mashantucket and the Paucatuck—had only about ten members each.

Did Indians sell Manhattan for a few beads?

When Dutch traders built a post at New Amsterdam (now New York City), they did give the Lenape Indians some beads and other trinkets worth about $24. The Lenape, however, did not consider this payment for their land. Like other Indian people, they did not think of land as something that could be bought and sold. They probably regarded the beads as a gift, a gesture meant to keep the Lenape friendly. In Indian cultures, gift-giving was a common way of cementing allegiances between peoples. The Dutch likely knew this custom, so they, too, probably considered the beads to be no more than a token of their goodwill.

What was wampum?

Wampum were small purple or white beads made from shells. These beads had great value to Indian tribes throughout the Northeast, particularly the Iroquois. The Iroquois believed that holding strings of wampum could give comfort to people grieving the loss of a loved one. They also wove wampum beads together to form belts to commemorate important events.

When non-Indian traders arrived in the Northeast, they quickly realized how much the Iroquois treasured

Kateri Tekakwitha

In the late 1600s, the French tried to build an allegiance with the powerful Iroquois. Part of their effort was to send Catholic priests of the Jesuit order to live among the Mohawk. The Jesuits wanted to convert the Indians to Christianity.

Most Mohawk people were leery of the priests, whom they called Black Robes because of the long, dark cloaks they wore. A few, however, embraced the new religion. The most passionate convert was Kateri Tekakwitha, the niece of an important Mohawk leader. Against her uncle's wishes, she devoted her short life to becoming a nun and serving the church. Since her death in 1680 at the age of 24, the Catholic Church has named her venerable and blessed—two of the three steps toward being declared a saint.

wampum and started making the beads to give to their new trading partners. For a time, in the fur trade, wampum was used like money.

What was the French and Indian War?

The French and Indian War was the last and most important in a series of wars fought between France and England in the eighteenth century. Both countries claimed some of the same lands in the Northeast, so they went to war to determine who would control the area. Although Indians had lived on these lands for centuries, neither country believed tribes had a claim to their own territory.

When the fighting broke out in 1754, each side asked its Indian allies for help. Although some Indians, such as the Mohawk led by Chief Hendrick, fought with the English, many more—including the Ojibwa, Ottawa, and Potawatomi—initially sided with the French because they generally treated Indians better. Unfortunately for their Indian allies, the French lost the war in 1763. After their victory, the British (and later the Americans) grew in numbers and overran more and more Indian territory in the Northeast.

Did Indians fight in the American Revolution?

Many Indians stayed neutral, because they disliked both the English and the American colonists rebelling against them. However, some groups, such as the six Iroquois tribes, took sides. When the war began in 1776, the influential Mohawk chief Joseph Brant allied his people with the English. The Onondaga, Seneca, and Cayuga followed his lead, but the Oneida and Tuscarora decided to fight on the side of the Americans. For the first time in the history of the Iroquois Confederacy, Iroquois of one tribe were fighting those of another.

In addition to nearly destroying the confederacy, the war caused the Iroquois to lose large amounts of land. Soon after the revolution ended in 1783 with an American victory, the United States took over much of their territory in what is now New York State. It even confiscated land from the Oneida and Tuscarora, who had helped the new country win the war.

Who was Tecumseh?

After the American Revolution, thousands of American settlers flooded into the Ohio River Valley, pushing tribes such as the Shawnee, Ojibwa, and Potawatomi out of their lands. Tecumseh was a Shawnee leader who believed these tribes needed to band together to fight the American intruders. He was inspired by the beliefs of his younger brother, Tenskwatawa. Tenskwatawa was a religious prophet who preached that Americans were the children of

A Deadly Game of Lacrosse

During the French and Indian War, a group of Great Lakes Indians led by the Ottawa leader Pontiac began attacking British forts in their territory. In one of the most notorious events of Pontiac's War, the Ojibwa staged a surprise raid on Fort Michilimackinac on present-day Mackinac Island, Michigan.

With the permission of the British, a team of Ojibwa men had gathered to play lacrosse, an ancient Indian sport on the grounds just outside the fort. During the game, a player "accidentally" tossed the ball over the fort's high walls. Several Ojibwa rushed into the stockade as though they were trying to retrieve the ball. Once inside, they pulled guns on the stunned soldiers. Catching their enemies completely off guard, the warriors were able to kill the fort commander and take several soldiers hostage.

the evil Great Serpent and that Indians should end all contact with them. A great speaker, Tecumseh traveled through present-day Ohio, Michigan, Indiana, and Illinois asking the Indians there to join his confederacy.

Did Tecumseh's confederacy succeed?

Tecumseh and Tenskwatawa rallied many Indians to their cause. But while Tecumseh was journeying through the Southeast looking for more support, the confederacy was dealt a serious blow. Troops led by William Henry Harrison attacked and destroyed Tippecanoe—the town that served as Tecumseh and Tenskwatawa's headquarters.

Tecumseh's forces continued to fight until October 1813, when Harrison once again met Tecumseh's followers at the Battle of the Thames. During the fighting, Tecumseh was killed. Without his leadership, his warriors became disorganized, and Tecumseh and Tenskwatawa's dream of a united Indian nation faded.

What happened to northeastern Indians after Tecumseh's defeat?

As Americans flooded into tribes' traditional homelands, many Indians lost their lands and were forced to move west. One example were the Wyandot, a branch of the Huron tribe. In the early nineteenth century, they were living in Ohio and Michigan. In 1843 the United States moved them to present-day Kansas so their lands could be opened up to whites. After only 14 years, they were on the move again, heading to present-day Oklahoma to escape from the non-Indians settling in their Kansas territory.

Some tribes, though, were able to stay in the lands of their ancestors. The Iroquois, for instance, held on to several reservations in New York State, although this land was only a fraction of their original territory. The Menominee and Potawatomi also retained much of their territory in the Great Lakes region, largely because their lands were so swampy that few white settlers and farmers wanted to live there.

While tribes struggled to hold on to their lands, they also found their traditional ways threatened. Increasingly, government officials and Christian missionaries pressured

Indians to live more like whites. Many Indians, even those on reservations, slowly abandoned some Indian ways and adopted some white customs. For example, the famous Mohawk poet Emily Pauline Johnson (1861–1913) grew up in a mansion and went to an English-run school for wealthy girls. Even though her upbringing was more like that of a white upper-class lady than a traditional Mohawk woman, she retained her pride in her Indian heritage, which provided the subject for her best works.

Who is Ada Deer?

In the 1970s, a young Menominee woman named Ada Deer decided to take on the U.S. government to save her tribe's land. In 1970, the Menominee had become the first tribe to lose its reservation due to a government policy known as termination. The goal of termination was to dissolve reservations so that the government could save the money it spent on maintaining them.

As the vice president of the National Committee to Save the Menominee People and Forest, Deer traveled to Washington, D.C., and spoke before Congress. In passionate speeches, she explained how termination violated the United States's promise in an 1854 treaty that her tribe would have their reservation forever. Largely because of her efforts, the government at last admitted its mistake. President Richard M. Nixon signed the Menominee Restoration Act of 1973, which gave the Menominee their reservation back.

In 1992 Deer was named the assistant secretary of the Bureau of Indian Affairs, the U.S. government agency that deals with Native American tribes. She became the first Native American woman ever to hold this important post.

Do any Native Americans still live in the northeast?

Today, Native Americans live throughout the Northeast. Some make their home in tribal communities on reservations, such as the Penobscot Reservation in Maine and the Mashantucket Pequot Reservation in Connecticut. Most, however, live in towns and cities where the majority of residents are non-Indians. With a Native American population of 63,000, New York is the northeastern state with

In 1840 William Henry Harrison and John Tyler were elected president and vice-president. Their campaign slogan—"Tippecanoe and Tyler, too"—reminded voters of Harrison's victory over Tecumseh's forces in the Battle of Tippecanoe.

Building the Skyline

Many of the first huge sky-scrapers in the United States and Canada were built by Mohawk Indians. Mohawk men were first hired as steelworkers in 1886 during the construction of a bridge across the St. Lawrence River. Because of their fearlessness in climbing the high beams, construction companies soon sought out Mohawk workers to work on other steel structures throughout the country. New York City's Empire State Building and San Francisco's Golden Gate Bridge are just two of the modern wonders Mohawk have helped create.

the largest number of Native Americans. Close behind is the Great Lakes state of Michigan, where 56,000 Native Americans live.

Because northeastern Indians were the first to have extensive contact with non-Indians, they lost more of their lands and traditions than tribes in many areas of North

Iroquois Indians John Tarbell, Joe La Claire, Jack Hill, and Peter Horn (from left to right) migrated south to New York City from the Kanamake reservation in Canada. Like many other Mohawk and Iroquois Indians from that area, they found work in high-rise steel construction.

America. Yet, through remarkable determination, many of their ways and beliefs have survived. The Ojibwa still revere the secrets of Midewiwin, the Menominee continue to harvest the wild rice that has always nourished their people, and, 500 years after its founding, the great Iroquois Confederacy still stands strong.

AMERICAN INDIANS OF THE SOUTHEAST

Which tribes originally lived in the Southeast?

The center of the Southeast—including what are now the states of Tennessee, Georgia, Alabama, and Mississippi—was the home of many large Indian groups, such as the Cherokee, the Chickasaw, the Choctaw, and the Creek confederacy of tribes. To their east lived the Tuscarora of present-day North Carolina, the Catawba and the Yamasee of what is now South Carolina, and the Timucua of present-day Florida. To their west were the Biloxi and the Tunica of present-day Louisiana and the Natchez of what is now southern Mississippi.

Why did so many large tribes live in the Southeast?

The Southeast had plenty of fertile land, so the Indians there became expert farmers. Both men and women prepared the fields and brought in the harvest. But most of the planting and the day-to-day tending was the responsibility of women. By growing vegetables, they could feed many people, but they had to stay near their fields if they were going to care for the crops properly. Southeastern peoples, therefore, tended to live in large, settled villages. As many as 90 of these villages clustered together formed a tribe.

What was the most important crop for southeastern Indian tribes?

They grew many crops—including beans, potatoes, peas, and pumpkins—but the most important was corn.

While fasting during the Green Corn Ceremony, men drank Black Drink. This special tea, brewed from the leaves of a holly plant, was thought to take away peoples' anger and make them speak truthfully.

Women knew how to cook dozens of delicious dishes—from corn mush to corn bread—from this staple food. By drying much of their crop, they also made sure that their families would have plenty of corn to eat long after the summer harvest. Women crafted huge storage baskets to keep the corn dry and protected from animals throughout the winter months.

What was the Green Corn Ceremony?

The Green Corn Ceremony was a great festival held by most Southeast tribes to celebrate the ripening of the year's corn crop. In late summer, leaders from the host village sent out the word of when and where the ceremony would be held. Friends and relatives from neighboring villages would then gather, helping each other build temporary dwellings and clear an area for dancing and feasting.

Timucua Indian hunters attack an alligator in this German engraving, printed in 1590, about 50 years after Europeans first encountered Southeastern Indians. The artist drew the alligator much larger than it probably was. Europeans were fascinated by the peoples of the Americas, but few early depictions of them were accurate.

The Pottery of the Catawba

For more than 4,000 years, Catawba women have made beautiful pottery using the same technique. A potter first shapes a ball of clay into a pancakelike base. She then rolls more clay into tubes, which she coils around the base and flattens out to form the pot's walls. After the pot dries, its surface is smoothed with a stone. The potter then places the pot into a pit of fire. The firing process gives the pot a smooth finish and makes the clay take on the mixture of orange, brown, and black colors for which Catawba pottery is known.

For the first one or two days of the ceremony, men stopped eating in order to purify their bodies. During this time, they met in a council to discuss problems in their villages and decide the fates of criminals. The fast was broken when the host village's shaman, or medicine man, lit the "breath master," a ceremonial fire. After extinguishing all the cooking fires in the village, women took hot coals from the breath master and used them to relight the flames. The event symbolized the end of the old year and beginning of the new.

A great feast followed, during which everyone enjoyed ears of sweet, fresh corn after months of eating dried corn from the previous year's harvest. Dancing and singing, the people were filled with goodwill. They renewed old friendships, forgave past wrongs, and gave thanks to the creator for the new year ahead.

Did southeastern tribes get all their food from farming?

Southeast Indians also ate meat, fish, and wild plants. Men hunted animals that lived in the forests that covered much of the Southeast. Using spears or bows and arrows, they stalked large game, such as deer and bear. For hunting rabbits, squirrels, and other small animals, they usually set traps, then used a club to kill the animals they caught. Some tribes also used blowguns to shoot darts at small prey. Men also fished in rivers and lakes, while women gathered a wide variety of nuts and berries that grew wild in the Southeast.

The homes of all southeastern Indians were made of wood, mud, and grass. However, the chickee—a house with open sides and a floor built several feet above the earth—was uniquely suited to the hot and swampy region where the Seminole lived.

What type of houses did southeastern Indians build?

Throughout the Southeast, Indians used the same materials—wood, mud, and dried grass—to build their houses. The type of dwelling, however, varied from tribe to tribe depending on the environment.

Tribes such as the Choctaw and Cherokee lived in areas that were very hot in the summer, but that could be cold and snowy during the short winter. These groups built two different houses—one for the hot weather and one for the cold. Their cone-shaped winter houses were made from a frame of wood and insulated with clay and mud. Their summer dwellings were rectangular wooden structures with gabled roofs of grass left open on the sides to allow air to circulate.

In hotter climates farther south, tribes such as the Seminole of Florida spent all year long in *chickees*. These were simple wooden houses with floors built several feet above the ground to protect the residents from snakes and swamp waters. *Chickees* had roofs made from the leaves of the palmetto tree, but they had no walls at all. Sitting in a *chickee*, a family was shaded from the hot sun but could still feel a cooling breeze.

What other structures were found in southeastern villages?

The houses in a village were built around a courtyard that was big enough to hold all the village residents and their guests during the Green Corn Ceremony and other important events. By the courtyard was a council house, where the wise old men and distinguished warriors who ruled the village could meet. Every village also had a great ball court. There, in summer, men gathered to play a spirited game they called *chunky* that was similar to the modern sport of lacrosse.

Who was Hernando de Soto?

Hernando de Soto was a Spanish explorer who came to the Southeast in 1539 looking for gold and other riches. He and his 600 men were the first non-Indians to meet most of the tribes there. The encounters were often violent. De Soto's men tried to kill or enslave many of the Indians they came upon, and the tribes fought back. De Soto's travels ended when he died in 1542. But news of his explorations and of the rich lands in the Southeast encouraged other non-Indians to follow. Over the next three centuries, white traders and settlers from Spain, England, and France steadily moved into southeastern Indian territory.

What was the Yamasee War?

In the early eighteenth century, the English established the colony of South Carolina on the territory of the Yamasee tribe. The colonists treated the Indians terribly. They stole their land and captured many Yamasee and sent them to the West Indies where they were sold as slaves. By 1715, the Yamasee had had enough. They attacked the English and tried to drive them from their lands. Other Indians, including many Creek, joined in the fight. The English coaxed the Cherokee, who had a tense relationship with the Creek, to battle for their side. In the end, the English won and the surviving Yamasee were forced to scatter and find new homes with other tribes.

A Beloved Woman

In 1755, during a war between the Cherokee and Creek, a woman named Nanye'hi followed her husband into battle to provide him with ammunition and encouragement. During the battle, her husband was shot. Without a moment's thought, Nanye'hi reached over his body, snatched his weapon, and took his place in the fight as she sang out a Cherokee war song to inspire her fellow warriors.

Because of her courage, the Cherokee honored Nanye'hi with the title Beloved Woman. As a Beloved Woman, Nanye'hi was able to go to meetings of the Cherokee Council, which was usually only attended by men. She was also given the vital duty of preparing Black Drink, the power-giving tea that men drank during ceremonies. Several years after the death of her Cherokee husband, Nanye'hi married an Irish trader named Brian Ward.

Trusted by both Cherokees and whites (who knew her as Nancy Ward), she became a celebrated peacemaker between the two groups. Today, Cherokees still honor Nancy Ward as a Beloved Woman who provided their people with sound and sane counsel.

Who were the Five Civilized Tribes?

The Cherokee, Chickasaw, Creek, Choctaw, and Seminole were called the Five Civilized Tribes by non-Indians. During the eighteenth century, these large tribes quickly developed friendly relationships with European trading partners. In time, many traders married into their tribes and introduced the Indians to white ways and values. Because the tribes adopted some of these customs, whites thought they were more civilized than other Indian peoples.

What was the Booger Dance?

In the winter, the Cherokee enjoyed a rowdy cere-mony called the Booger Dance. After guests arrived at the host's home, four masked dancers ran into the house. The dancers, called boogers, made crude noises and chased women around the room, all for the amusement of the audience. The masks of the boogers had grotesque features and often depicted non-Indians. The dance may have started as a way of making fun of these intruders in the Cherokee homeland.

Who was Sequoyah?

Born in about 1770, Sequoyah was a Cherokee man who invented a way of writing down the Cherokee's spoken language. The task was very difficult: He worked for years alone in a cabin, making marks on scraps of paper and wood chips. Many of his friends made fun of him. His wife even burned down his cabin to make him stop his work. Although many of his early writing experiments were destroyed in the fire, Sequoyah was so determined that he just started working again.

At first, Sequoyah tried creating one symbol to stand for every Cherokee word, but this system was too complicated. He then decided to use symbols to represent each sound in the Cherokee language. Sequoyah came up with 85 symbols, which he taught to his daughter Ahyokeh. To introduce his writing system to other Cherokee, Sequoyah and Ahyokeh gave public demonstrations during which they took turns deciphering messages written using Sequoyah's symbols.

Why was Sequoyah's written language important?

Sequoyah's writing system was so simple that a Cherokee speaker could master reading and writing in a few days. Almost overnight, the Cherokee became a literate people. Suddenly, they could write down their laws and history, record information about medicines, healing techniques, and business transactions, and communicate with friends and relatives who were far away.

Sequoyah said he valued his written language because it unburdened his memory, freeing his mind to think of other things. As he once said, "When I have heard anything, I write it down, and lay it by and take it up again at some future day. And there find all that I have heard exactly as I heard it."

What was removal?

By the early nineteenth century, non-Indian settlers were clamoring for the rich, fertile lands where Southeast Indians lived. With the support of President Andrew Jackson, they demanded that the U.S. government force the Indians to leave the region once and for all. The

In the eighteenth century, some wealthy southeastern Indians adopted the white custom of owning African American slaves.

In 1828, the Cherokees began publishing the first Indian newspaper, the Cherokee Phoenix. *It printed the news in English and in Cherokee using Sequoyah's writing system.*

result was a policy called removal, defined in the Indian Removal Act of 1830. In this law, Congress authorized officials to make treaties with southeastern tribes, in which the tribes could agree to give their territory to the United States in exchange for new lands west of the Mississippi River. These treaties were rarely negotiated with the actual leaders of the tribes. For instance, after the Cherokee's chiefs stormed out of the treaty negotiations vowing never to sign a removal treaty, the officials turned to a few proremoval Cherokee. These Indians signed the treaty, even though they had no power or right to speak for their tribe.

What was Indian Territory?

Indian Territory was the name given to the western lands where the United States wanted to resettle the southeastern Indians. Originally, it did not have exact boundaries, but by the late nineteenth century the area was defined roughly as what is now the state of Oklahoma.

Sequoyah is depicted holding his invention: the Cherokee syllabary. It consists of 85 symbols derived in part from English, Greek, and Hebrew characters. A brilliant man, Sequoyah is the only person in history to invent an entire method of writing by himself.

How did Indians feel about the removal policy?

The Indians of the Southeast hated the idea of removal. Their entire way of life and religion was tied to their homelands—the places where their ancestors had lived and were buried. They knew little about Indian Territory, except that it was already occupied by Indians, such as the Kiowa and Pawnee, with very different ways. As settled farmers, the southeastern Indians were wary of the Indians in the west, whose societies were built around hunting and warring.

Some groups, such as the Creek and Seminole, fought to stay in their lands. Others, like the Cherokee, tried to negotiate with the U.S. government to retain their southeastern territory. Despite their efforts, during the 1830s, many southeastern Indians were compelled, often by force, to move west.

What was the Seminole Resistance?

Originally part of the Creek, the Seminole fled their homeland in present-day Georgia and Alabama when settlers began overtaking their lands in the 1700s. Along with Indians from other tribes, such as the Yamasee, and some escaped African American slaves, the Seminole formed a new tribe in what is now Florida.

The Seminole strongly opposed the U.S. government's plan to make them leave the Southeast. Led by the great warrior Osceola, they went to war with the United States to stop their removal. The Seminole battled U.S. troops from 1835 to 1842. During the years of fighting, the United States succeeded in forcing about 3,000 Seminoles to move west to Indian Territory. But about 500 tribe members, hiding in the Florida swamps, were so resistant that the army finally gave up the fight. Today, there are two branches of the tribe: one in Oklahoma (formerly Indian Territory) and one in the Seminole's Florida homeland.

What was the Trail of Tears?

"Trail of Tears" is the English translation of Nunna Daul Tsunyi, the name the Cherokee gave to their long journey to Indian Territory in 1838. This disaster began when U.S. troops stormed Cherokee villages and destroyed

"The Trail of Tears" was an appropriate name for the Cherokee's journey to Indian Territory, where the United States wanted the tribe to resettle. Not only did the Cherokee leave against their wishes, but also as many as one-fourth of the people who began the journey did not survive.

their crops, property, and homes. The soldiers then forcibly rounded up the Cherokee people and placed them in concentration camps while the government planned their relocation.

The United States had promised to supply the relocating Cherokee with food and other supplies, but U.S. officials stole most of the provisions intended for the tribe. With almost nothing to eat, the Cherokee were sent off on the long, deadly walk to their new homeland. Along the way, many people, especially the very young and very old, fell victim to starvation and disease. About one out of every four people on the Trail of Tears died before reaching Indian Territory.

Other southeastern Indian tribes had their own "trail of tears." The Choctaw, Creek, Chickasaw, and Seminole also suffered terribly during their trek to Indian Territory.

Did any Indians stay in the Southeast?

Some Indians from removed tribes pledged to stay in the Southeast no matter what. Determined Seminole hid in the swamps, while Cherokee ran off into the mountains to avoid U.S. troops who wanted to force them off their land.

The land of some of the smaller southeastern tribes had already been so overrun by whites that the U.S. government never bothered to try to remove them. For instance, the Tunica of Mississippi and the Catawba of South Carolina were able to stay in their old territory in the Southeast.

How did the Civil War affect Indian Territory?

The Civil War began in 1861 when the states in the South (called the Confederacy) declared their independence from the states in the North (called the Union). Although Indians were not then citizens of the United States, the Confederacy pressured the Five Civilized Tribes to become its allies. Because they had originally lived in

A portrait by Charles Bird King shows William McIntosh, who signed a treaty on behalf of the Lower Creek giving the United States a large portion of Creek territory in exchange for a new homeland west of the Mississippi River. The Upper Creek did not agree with his action, and under a new tribal law, he was executed.

The Execution of William McIntosh

Indians in the same tribe often disagreed about how to deal with land-hungry Americans moving onto their lands. Among the Creek, a large southern tribe, one group—called the Upper Creek—wanted to fight the Americans. Another group—called the Lower Creek—believed they could not possibly win a war with the United States. They thought the best course of action was to sell their southeastern territory to the United States and move to a new homeland in the West.

The disagreement came to a head in 1825 with the Treaty of Indian Springs. In it, the Lower Creek agreed to give the United States a large area of Creek land in Georgia and Alabama. They were led by William McIntosh, who several times before had tried to keep the peace by turning over Creek territory to the U.S. government.

By signing the treaty, McIntosh not only infuriated the Upper Creek. He also broke a new Creek law that sentenced to death any person who sold or gave away Creek land. After the treaty signing, a force of 170 Creek warriors was sent to capture McIntosh. A traitor to some, a hero to others, he was hanged on the morning of May 12, 1825.

During the American Civil War, the Cherokee nearly had one of their own. One group of tribe members, led by Stand Watie, supported the South, and another, led by John Ross, wanted to stay neutral. The dispute ended only after Ross was forced to back down.

the South, they had closer ties to the Confederacy than to the Union.

Not all Indians in Indian Territory, however, wanted to join the Confederacy. Some Indians fought with the Union forces. Many who did had first joined the Confederate army, but decided to switch sides when they grew disillusioned with the Confederacy. Others wanted to fight for the Union only after they were attacked by Confederate troops.

Fighting on both sides, Indians were often pitted against Indians as the war ripped through Indian Territory. The experience was so devastating that, a month after the war ended with a Union victory, 14 tribes signed a declaration, agreeing that they would no longer shed each others' blood.

What happened to the Confederate Indians when the South lost?

The Civil War was a disaster for the Indians of Indian Territory. Some 10,000 of them were killed during the war.

So many homes and fields were looted and burned that many survivors were left with nothing.

Adding to these Indians' troubles, the United States pushed the Cherokee, Creek, Seminole, Choctaw, and Chickasaw—the tribes who had allied themselves to the Confederacy—to sign peace treaties meant to punish the Indian rebels. The U.S. government forced them to sell their lands in the western half of Indian Territory and made them agree to let the government build railroads through their nations. It also directed the Indians to free their slaves and make them tribe members.

Did Indian Territory become a state?

No, but after the Civil War, many Indian leaders wanted it to. They proposed that it join the Union as an Indian state called Sequoyah, after the famous inventor of the Cherokee writing system. The U.S. government ignored the request. It now wanted to open the Indian Territory for white settlement.

In 1890 the western half of Indian Territory was renamed Oklahoma Territory. After that area was settled by non-Indians, the government merged Indian Territory and Oklahoma Territory in 1907 to create the state of Oklahoma. Despite enormous resistance by Indian Territory leaders, the

During the Civil War, the population of the Cherokee, Creek, and Seminole tribes dropped nearly 25 percent because of war-related deaths.

In 1984, 10,000 Cherokee came together in Red Clay, Tennessee, to attend a joint tribal council. It was the first council with leaders from both branches of the Cherokee since the Trail of Tears broke up the tribe almost 150 years earlier.

"I Love My Home"

In 1834, rebel Seminole leader Osceola used these words to rally his people to fight to stay in their homeland:

The [government] agent tells us we must go away from the lands we live on—our homes, and the graves of our Fathers, and go over the big river [the Mississippi] among the bad Indians. When the agent tells me to go from my home, I hate him, because I love my home, and will not go from it.

My Brothers! When the Great Spirit tells me to go with the white man, I go: but he tells me not to go. The white man says I shall go, and he will send people to make me go; but I have a rifle, and I have some powder and some lead. I say, we must not leave our homes and lands. If any of our people want to go west, we won't let them; and I tell them they are our enemies, and we will treat them so, for the Great Spirit will protect us.

Seminole Patchwork

In the late nineteenth century, whites introduced the sewing machine to the Seminole—an event that sparked an entirely new art form. Seminole women took to patchworking long horizontal bands of cloth. They then sewed these bands together to make brilliantly patterned shirts and skirts. Although most Seminole now dress in the same type of clothes as non-Indians, they still make colorful patchwork outfits to wear for special occasions.

United States, in preparation for statehood, dissolved the Indian nations in Indian Territory. Their governments' were disbanded and their tribal lands were broken up into small plots owned by individual Indians.

What happened to the Indian Territory tribes?

When Indian Territory became part of Oklahoma, the United States declared that the Indian nations there no longer existed. The government wanted the Indians to blend into white society and forget their ancestors' ways. Many Indians did come to live much like their white neighbors, but they never forgot they were Indians. They retained their traditions, honored their ancestors, and taught their children what it meant to be members of their tribe.

In 1936, the United States set forth guidelines by which the Oklahoma tribes could re-form their tribal governments. These new governments have helped tribes revive many of their traditional ways. Many people have also retained ties to Indian relatives whose ancestors stayed in the Southeast. Through these relationships, tribe members have kept alive a close connection to their old southeastern homeland.

What are the Great Plains? ◆ Which Indian groups
lived on the Plains? ◆ When did Indians come to the
region? ◆ D ? ◆ Why
were horses so important to Plains Indians? ◆ What
was a tipi? ◆ How did Plains Indians hunt buffalo? ◆
What was a sweat lodge? ◆ What was the Sun Dance?
◆ Were Plains Indians warlike? ◆ Why did men become
warriors? ◆ What weapons did they use? ◆ Who were
the leaders in Plains tribes? ◆ What work did Plains
Indian women do? ◆ When did Plains Indians come
in contact with whites? ◆ What was Red Cloud's War?
◆ Why did the U.S. government want Plains Indians

AMERICAN INDIANS OF THE PLAINS

What are the Great Plains?

The Great Plains are a vast area of flat, grassy land in the center of North America. East to west, the plains stretch from the Mississippi River Valley to the Rocky Mountains. North to south, they extend from the Canadian provinces of Alberta, Saskatchewan, and Manitoba down to central Texas.

Which Indian groups lived on the Plains?

The three branches of the Sioux (Lakota, Dakota, and Nakota), Cheyenne, Arapaho, and Pawnee lived in the central plains. To the south were the Comanche, Kiowa, and Apache. To the north were the Blackfeet, Hidatsa, and Mandan.

When did Indians come to the region?

The Indian groups such as the Sioux, Cheyenne, and Apache that we most associate with the Great Plains started to arrive there in about 1650. They came to the Plains from the east and north after being pushed out of their lands by other Indians who had been forced from their own territories by whites. Before coming to the Plains, they had lived by growing crops, gathering wild plants, and hunting small animals. In their new home, however, they flourished by becoming buffalo hunters.

The Indians of the Plains spoke many different languages. When trading with one another, they used an elaborate sign language to communicate.

More than 150 years after they were created, George Catlin's paintings provide glimpses into Native American life. Here the artist shows a pair of Plains Indians sneaking up on a herd of buffalo. The wolf skins disguised the hunters until they could get close enough to use their spears.

Did Plains Indians always ride horses?

Small prehistoric horses once lived in North America, but they died out about 10,000 years ago. The Plains Indians did not have the type of horse we know now until Spaniards brought them to America from Europe in the sixteenth century. Spanish horses that escaped their keepers formed wild herds. By 1780, Plains Indians were skilled at capturing and taming these animals. They found the horse so useful that soon their entire way of life revolved around this animal.

Why were horses so important to Plains Indians?

By riding horses, Indians could travel from place to place faster than ever before. A mounted hunter or warrior had an enormous advantage over slow-moving prey or an unmounted enemy. He could even pursue stampeding buffalo and follow herds of these beasts wherever they roamed in any kind of weather. By allowing them to hunt buffalo much of the year, the horse ensured that the Indians would have plenty of meat to eat and enough hides to make their clothing and tipis.

What was a tipi?

A tipi, which consisted of a hide cover placed over a wooden frame, was the dwelling favored by the Plains Indians. For a people who spent most of their time on the move, the tipi was a perfect type of house—light to carry and easy to assemble and disassemble whenever necessary. The hide tipi covers also offered Indian artists a large surface to decorate. The covers were usually painted by men with pictures that boasted about their exploits in battle. Sometimes they featured patterns at the top that were identified with a certain family. These patterns could be seen from a long distance away and therefore acted as signals to let relatives know where their kin were camping.

How did Plains Indians hunt buffalo?

Before Plains Indians had horses, they hunted buffalo on foot. A hunter often draped himself in the skin of a wolf to trick a buffalo into letting him get close enough to stab the animal with a spear.

Hunting on horseback was much easier. Traveling with their families in small bands, hunters with horses could go wherever buffalo herds went. Riding alongside their prey, they used bows and arrows to shoot the mighty animals. On a well-trained horse, a hunter could get close enough to a running buffalo to kill it with a single arrow.

Another method of hunting buffalo was the jump-kill. By riding toward a herd screaming and yelling, a group of hunters steered the frightened buffalo off a cliff. Any animals that survived the fall were killed with spears by hunters waiting below. A successful jump-kill might kill 100 buffalo and yield tons of meat.

Blackfeet Indians named a favorite jump-kill site "Head-Smashed-In."

What was a sweat lodge?

A sweat lodge was a small dome-shaped structure made out of bent poles covered with hides. Men gathered in these structures as part of a religious ceremony. In the center of the sweat lodge they placed a pile of stones that had been heated in a fire. Pouring cold water over the stones, the participants filled the lodge with steam, causing them to perspire profusely. The sweat lodge ritual was thought to cleanse both the body and the spirit.

The All-Purpose Buffalo

The buffalo gave Indians far more than just meat. In fact, the animal provided them with almost everything they needed to live. The list below includes some of the many uses Indians had for the animal's different parts.

hides: tipi covers, clothing, storage bags, blankets, shield covers

fat: candles, soap

horns: spoons, bowls

bones: tools, arrowheads

bladders: containers

hair: ropes, headdresses, pillow stuffing

tendons: bow strings

hoofs: glue, ceremonial rattles, wind chimes

dung: fuel

brains: material for tanning hides

blood: paint, soup

teeth: ornaments

tongue: combs

intestines: cord

What was the Sun Dance?

The Sun Dance was a religious ceremony held by many Plains tribes. It lasted for three or four days, during which young men sang and danced to the sound of drums. The dancers did not eat or drink. Exhausted and hungry, they began to see visions.

The ceremony got its name from one part of the dance, in which dancers circled around a high pole stuck in the ground. Each dancer tied one end of a hide-string to the pole and attached the other end to wooden skewers inserted through holes punctured through the skin in their chest. Leaning back until the string was taut, the dancers stared into the sun. Eventually the string broke through their flesh and they fell to the ground. The ritual caused pain but no long-term physical damage. Through the Sun Dance, the Plains Indians felt they were able to communicate with the Creator and ask for the strength that would make them great warriors and leaders.

Were Plains Indians warlike?

Before they encountered non-Indians, young males of different tribes fought one another largely as a way of getting out their aggression. When non-Indians arrived on the Plains, however, warfare became more important. As non-Indians took over Indian land, they pushed out the tribes that lived there. These tribes then had to move into the lands of other Indians, who had to fight the newcomers to keep control over their territory.

Generally, a tribe's warriors fought against anyone who invaded their land or threatened their people—Indian or non-Indian. Some tribes, however, became long-standing enemies. The most intense rivalry on the Plains was between the Sioux and the Pawnee. The Pawnee's hatred of the Sioux was so intense that many joined the U.S. Army as scouts during the United States's military campaign against the Sioux in the late nineteenth century.

Fighting an enemy was not the only goal of war expeditions. Often, warriors went on raids to steal horses and other valued possessions of their rivals. On raids, men sometimes also took captives, who in many cases became adopted members of the warriors' tribes.

Plains Indians kept calendars called winter counts. Drawn on a hide or piece of cloth, a winter count featured pictures that represented battles, disease outbreaks, and other important events in a tribe's history.

Why did men become warriors?

Young men on the Plains were eager to go to war. Battles were exciting, and they gave men the opportunity

An unusual 1892 photograph captures part of the Sun Dance ceremony. These celebrants are Blackfeet Indians from Canada. The young man in the center is circling the striped pole at left.

to prove themselves. A brave fighter, like a talented hunter, earned the respect of his people. On special occasions, warriors were expected to boast of their war exploits to remind others about their achievements.

To warriors, the ceremonies associated with war were almost as important as fighting and raiding. War dances were held before an expedition to give the warriors courage and after to celebrate a victory. In some tribes, the most promising warriors were asked to join warrior societies, which performed ceremonies to ensure the tribe's well-being. During their initiation, young men learned about the societies' secret dances, songs, and symbols, as war leaders instructed them in the virtues of courage and self-control.

What weapons did they use?

Before they obtained guns from whites, Plains warriors fought their enemies in close combat with heavy war clubs or from a distance with bows and arrows tipped with stone points. Another popular weapon was the lance—a spear with a shaft as long as ten feet that a man on horseback could use to stab an opponent. Warriors also often carried shields. They painted their shields' hide coverings with designs or animal images that the warriors believed gave them special power in battle.

Who were the leaders in Plains tribes?

Although warriors were highly respected, the most important leaders on the Plains were chiefs. Chiefs were usually older men distinguished by their wisdom, fairness, and sense of honor. Each tribe had several chiefs who gathered together in council to make major decisions, such as whether to go to war. Chiefs also dealt with the day-to-day problems of their people. They determined when to go on a buffalo hunt, settled minor disputes between families, and made sure that the wives and children of fallen warriors were taken care of.

What work did Plains Indian women do?

Except in rare cases, women were not chiefs, warriors, or hunters. But women's work was very important to their tribes. When their men killed buffalo, women took over the task of skinning the huge animals. They were responsible, too, for the hard work of cooking and preserving the meat and preparing and sewing the hides so they could be used as tipi covers and clothing. In addition, they had to rear the tribe's children, set up and take down tipis as their families moved from place to place, and add to the food supply by gathering wild berries and roots.

Plains Indians sometimes carried their possessions on a travois, a wooden frame strapped to the shoulders of a dog. A strong dog could pull a travois packed with as much as 75 pounds of goods.

When did Plains Indians come in contact with whites?

In the early 1800s, non-Indian traders and trappers began arriving in the Plains. Indians generally welcomed these men, who supplied them with metal tools, guns, and other manufactured goods in exchange for animal hides.

The Plains Indians were less hospitable toward whites who in the 1840s started traveling through the Plains on their way to the rich farmland in present-day Oregon or goldfields in California and Montana. As the whites' wagons rattled across the Plains, they frightened away the buffalo. To drive away the trespassers on their land, war parties started attacking the wagons and stealing the settlers' supplies.

What was Red Cloud's War?

The Bozeman Trail was a route through Plains Indian territory that non-Indians followed to goldfields in present-day Montana and Colorado. To protect Americans traveling on the Bozeman Trail, the U.S. Army built three forts in Lakota territory. The Lakota Sioux, especially a young war chief named Red Cloud, were furious. Red Cloud and his warriors attacked the forts again and again. They were so determined that the U.S. government finally gave up the fight.

In 1868, the United States called a great council of Sioux leaders at Fort Laramie, an old trading post. There, the Sioux agreed to a peace treaty, in which the United States promised to abandon the Bozeman forts. It also created a large Sioux reservation—an area reserved exclusively for the Sioux where no whites would be allowed to settle.

Why did the U.S. government want Plains Indians to live on reservations?

If Indians were confined to a reservation, government officials could keep an eye on them more easily. The government also wanted to encourage Plains Indians to settle permanently on reservation lands and take up farming. Indians who farmed needed much less land than those who moved from place to place hunting buffalo. Plains Indian men, however, had little interest in becoming farmers. They found the work of farming hard and boring in comparison to the excitement of buffalo hunting.

What was the Dakota Uprising in Minnesota?

In 1851 the Dakota Sioux of what is now Minnesota signed a treaty in which they agreed to settle on a reservation. But soon they regretted the decision. The United States made the Dakota many promises in the treaty but kept none of them. Without the food and supplies the U.S. government was supposed to give them, the Indians faced starvation.

Angry and desperate, the Dakota led by Little Crow launched a full-scale war against their white neighbors in 1862. Before they were defeated by state troops, the rebels killed more than 500 whites. After the rebellion, 300 Indians were tried and sentenced to death, although President Abraham Lincoln reduced the sentence of all but 38. These Indians were hanged on December 26, 1863, in the biggest mass execution in U.S. history.

What are the Black Hills?

Indians called trains "iron horses."

The Black Hills are a group of rugged mountains along the border of South Dakota and Wyoming. The area was

Counting Coup

In Plains Indian culture, a warrior's greatest honor came from counting coup. He scored a coup by touching an enemy but otherwise leaving him unharmed. The Indians believed that a coup robbed an enemy of his spirit by shaming him. The more coup a warrior could claim, the more respect he commanded from his people.

Warrior Women

Although most Plains warriors were men, some women broke tradition by earning fame and honor on the battlefield. Brown Weasel Woman of the Blackfeet was such a successful horse raider and war-party leader that she was called Running Eagle, a name given to only the greatest Blackfeet fighters.

Woman Chief of the Crow was educated by her father as though she were his son. He taught her to use a bow and arrow, shoot a gun, and hunt on horseback and on foot. As an adult, Woman Chief emerged as a respected and wealthy Crow warrior and the only female member of the tribe's council of chiefs.

sacred to several Plains tribes, including the Lakota Sioux and the Cheyenne. According to Lakota legend, human beings lived under the mountains before they emerged to the surface of the earth. Because of their special connection to the Black Hills region, the Lakota call it "the heart of everything that is."

By the terms of the 1868 Treaty of Fort Laramie, the Black Hills were part of the Sioux's reservation. But only six years later, the region was invaded by a U.S. Army expedition headed by Lieutenant Colonel George Armstrong Custer. After the Custer expedition discovered gold there, white miners flooded into the Black Hills. Although by treaty the area was reserved for the Lakota, the U.S. government did almost nothing to keep whites from overrunning the Indians' most sacred site.

Who fought at the Battle of Little Bighorn?

Many Lakota Sioux refused to stay on their reservation and, angry at their treatment by whites, some raided non-Indian settlements. In 1876 the U.S. Army sent troops to subdue any Lakota bands who refused to live within reservation borders.

On June 25, soldiers again led by Custer attacked a group of Lakota and Cheyenne camped along the Little Bighorn River in Montana. In defending the camp, the Indians killed Custer and all of his men and chased away reinforcements sent to assist the troops. For the Indians, the battle was a great victory. For the army, it was a humiliating

Crazy Horse

Crazy Horse (1842–1877) was considered one of the Lakota Sioux's bravest and most intelligent warriors and raiders. He may have earned his name because he sometimes rammed his horse into that of an enemy to make his opponent fall to the ground. Widely respected by the young warriors of his tribe, he led them to victory in many battles, including the Battle of Little Bighorn of 1876. Following that conflict, the U.S. Army launched a vicious military campaign to punish the Lakota and their Cheyenne allies. Worn down by the attacks, Crazy Horse surrendered to U.S. troops on May 6, 1877. Defiant even in defeat, he angrily threw his weapons at the soldier's feet to show he was through with fighting. Fearful that the influential leader would organize an uprising, reservation police arrested and jailed Crazy Horse on September 5. In a scuffle, the great Crazy Horse was stabbed by a guard, and he died later that night.

defeat that made the soldiers determined to crush the renegade Indians once and for all.

Who was Sitting Bull?

Born in about 1831, Sitting Bull was perhaps the most respected leader of the Lakota Sioux during their war with the U.S. Army in the late nineteenth century. His people's faith in his courage and judgment was clear in their decision to name him head chief of all the Lakota in 1867, when he was only 36 years old. After fighting in the Battle of Little Bighorn in 1876, Sitting Bull took his followers to Canada to escape the vengeance of the U.S. troops. They stayed there for several harsh, cold winters that left them close to starvation. To save his people, Sitting Bull hesitantly returned to the United States in 1881 and agreed to live on a reservation. There he continued to be a leader, rallying his people to oppose the harsh rules of reservation officials and to keep their own ways alive. Branded as a troublemaker, Sitting Bull was arrested on December 12, 1890. Three days later, he was shot and killed while in police custody.

Who was Quanah Parker?

Quanah Parker (c.1853–1911) was one of the Comanche's greatest leaders. Born in about 1853, he first made his mark as a warrior in the Comanche's campaigns against the U.S. Army, which wanted to confine his people to a reservation. Outnumbered, Parker and his followers surrendered in 1875. On the reservation, Parker emerged as a shrewd negotiator. He brought money into his tribe by leasing their lands to Texas cattlemen and often outsmarted U.S. officials who were trying to reduce the size of the reservation. Parker was also a passionate supporter of peyoteism (later known as the Native American Church), an Indian religion that developed on the Plains in the late nineteenth century.

What was Buffalo Bill's Wild West Show?

Buffalo Bill's Wild West Show was an elaborate spectacle of sharpshooting, trick riding, and dramatic re-creations of events in American history, particularly well-known battles between the U.S. Army and Plains Indians. Buffalo Bill (the stage name for William F. Cody) was a former U.S. Army scout and Indian fighter who found his true calling as an entertainer. His famous show toured all over the United States and Europe in the late nineteenth century.

An action-filled drawing depicts the Indian victory at the Battle at Little Big Horn.

The Legend of Cynthia Parker

One of the greatest legends of the West is the story of Cynthia Parker. In 1836, when she was only nine, the white pioneer girl was taken captive by Comanche warriors who raided her family's settlement in Texas. Following Comanche custom, she was adopted into the tribe. Her new Comanche parents renamed her Preloch. As she grew up, whites tried to convince the Comanches to release Preloch, but the tribe refused. Preloch loved her new family and did not want to leave. She eventually married a Comanche warrior, and they had three children.

In 1860 the U.S. Army attacked Preloch's camp while her husband and the other men were away. She was taken prisoner and sent to live with her white relatives. Although whites believed she had been "rescued," Preloch was heartbroken at being separated from her Comanche relatives. She died ten years later in misery. Her only surviving child, Quanah, grew up to be one of the greatest leaders of her tribe.

One of the biggest draws of the show was the Indians whom Cody hired as performers. Among them was the great Lakota chief Sitting Bull. In eastern towns and cities, most of Buffalo Bill's customers had never seen an Indian before. All they knew of tribes firsthand came from his sensational shows, which presented Indians as wild savages whom whites needed to conquer and tame. By spreading this false idea of Plains Indians, Buffalo Bill's entertainment helped gather popular support for the U.S. Army's brutal war against these peoples.

What happened to the buffalo of the Plains?

In the mid-1800s, white hunters started using rifles to kill buffalo for their hides, which could be sold for a high profit. Soon whites were killing many more buffalo than Indians were. And unlike the Indians, who used virtually every part of the buffalo, whites took only the skin and left the rest of the carcass behind to rot.

Because of these careless hunting practices, the enormous herds, once numbering more than 60,000,000 animals, quickly shrank. By the end of the nineteenth century, there were only a few hundred wild buffalo left on the Plains. The slaughter of the buffalo herds was a terrible blow to Plains Indians, because so many of their traditional activities and values revolved around buffalo hunting.

How did Indians cope with the end of their traditional way of life?

Settling on reservations, some Indians tried to farm and adopt other non-Indians ways as whites wanted them to do. Others fell into a deep depression or in desperation turned to alcohol. Still others, though, looked for comfort in new Indian religions. The most popular of these revolved around the Ghost Dance.

What was the Ghost Dance?

The Ghost Dance religion was founded in 1899 by Wovoka, a Northern Paiute prophet living in western Nevada. Wovoka told his followers that one day while chopping wood he fell dead and traveled to heaven. There he talked to God, who told him that Indians should live peacefully and perform the Round Dance, a ceremonial dance of his tribe.

The religion quickly spread to tribes such as the Arapaho, the Cheyenne, and the Sioux. Among these Plains Indians, it became known as the Ghost Dance. The religion's popularity among the Lakota Sioux of the South

These Arapaho were performing the Ghost Dance inspired by the vision of Wovoka, when anthropologist James Mooney took this picture.

The Fort Marion Drawings

In 1875 U.S. soldiers arrested 72 warriors—mostly Kiowa, Cheyenne, and Arapaho—whom the army thought were the most dangerous Indians of the southern Plains. To keep these men from influencing other Indians, the government sent them to Fort Marion, a prison in St. Augustine, Florida, thousands of miles from their homelands. During their three years in prison, the Fort Marion inmates were given pencils and paper, which they used to draw pictures for sale to non-Indian tourists.

Before the arrival of whites on the Plains, Indian artists did not have these art tools. They were accomplished painters, however, who used vegetable dyes to make pictures on animal hides. The Fort Marion artists used the same simple lines and figures favored by hide painters to tell the story of their lives in Florida and their long, difficult journey there. Through their drawings, they also recorded their treasured memories of their past lives as hunters and fighters on the Plains.

Dakota's Pine Ridge Indian Reservation particularly terrified whites in the area. The government agent responsible for overseeing the Pine Ridge Indians ordered them never to perform the Ghost Dance again. When they refused, he asked the U.S. government to send in soldiers to force them to stop.

Why did the Ghost Dance frighten whites?

In Wovoka's vision, God said that Indians should make peace with whites. But the version of his religion practiced by Plains Indians guaranteed that if the Indians performed the Ghost Dance, one day all whites would die. The Ghost Dancers' dead relatives would then come back to life, and all Indians would return to their old ways of life.

The message provided comfort to Indians who looked back longingly to the time when buffalo were plentiful and they alone ruled the Plains. Whites, though, could only see how eager the Ghost Dancers were to live in a world where all whites were dead. They were convinced that the religion's teachings would inspire Plains Indians to band together and attack white towns and settlements.

What happened at Wounded Knee?

In late December 1890, a group of Ghost Dancers, led by Big Foot, set off for the Pine Ridge agency. By voluntarily settling near the agency, Big Foot's Sioux Indian followers hoped to avoid an encounter with the U.S. Army.

During their journey, the Sioux camped along Wounded Knee Creek. There they were confronted by troops from the Seventh Cavalry. Cold, tired, and starving, the Indians immediately surrendered to the soldiers. Even though the Indians posed no threat to them, the troops treated the Ghost Dancers roughly.

The next morning, while the soldiers were grabbing at the Indians' weapons to disarm them, a shot went off. In a panic, the troops began shooting into the crowd, killing every Indian they could. They chased the survivors, firing at them as they fled for cover. When the shooting ended, the shores of Wounded Knee Creek were covered with the bodies of some 300 Indians. Most of the dead were women, children, and babies.

Who was the Lost Bird?

Four days after the Wounded Knee Massacre, crews arrived to bury the dead and search for survivors. Wandering through the woods, they heard a muffled wail. The cry came from a baby girl wrapped in the arms of her dead mother. On the infant's head was a tiny cap decorated with red, white, and blue beads sewn in the shape of an American flag.

Named Zintkala Nuni, meaning "lost bird," the orphan was adopted by Leonard W. Colby, a brigadier general in the U.S. Army. To Colby, the girl was little more than a living souvenir of Wounded Knee. His wife, Clara, however, loved the girl, even though Clara's efforts to force her to live like a non-Indian drove a wedge between them. Desperately unhappy, when she reached adulthood, Zintkala Nuni tried to find peace by living among the Lakota Sioux. But because she had been raised in a white family, they no longer considered her one of them. Unwelcome in both Indian and non-Indian society, Zintkala Nuni lived in despair until she died of influenza at 29.

A 1903 photograph shows Chief Joseph one year before his death on the Colville Reservation in eastern Washington State, where he and his Nez Perce followers were forced to settle. Twenty-seven years earlier, Chief Joseph had nearly led them to freedom in Canada.

In 1995 the sad life of Zintkala Nuni inspired Marie Not Help Him of the Wounded Knee Survivor's Association to found the Lost Bird Society. This organization offers support and guidance to Indians who have been adopted by non-Indian parents.

How did Indians respond to the Wounded Knee Massacre?

The horrible slaughter at Wounded Knee marked the end of the wars between Indians and the U.S. Army on the Plains. One of the most tragic events in all of American history, the massacre has been seen by Indians for the past 100 years as a symbol of the many injustices

"I Will Fight No More Forever"

One of the last chiefs to surrender to the U.S. government was Chief Joseph. Joseph was the leader of a band of Nez Perce, a plateau Indian tribe native to western Idaho and eastern Oregon. Rather than settle on a reservation, Joseph's band ran off toward Canada pursued by U.S. troops. Captured just 40 miles from the Canadian border, Joseph said these words as he surrendered on October 5, 1877:

"I am tired of fighting. Our chiefs are killed. Looking Glass is dead. Too-

hoolhoolzote is dead. The old men are all dead...It is cold and we have no blankets. The little children are freezing to death. My people, some of them, have run away to the hills, and have no blankets, no food; no one knows where they are—perhaps freezing to death. I want to have time to look for my children and see how many I can find. Maybe I shall find them among the dead. Hear me, my chiefs. I am tired; my heart is sick and sad. From where the sun now stands I will fight no more forever."

they have suffered. In the late 1960s and early 1970s, when many Indians began to protest against the American government, they often reminded non-Indians of the Wounded Knee Massacre to show how badly Indians had been treated.

Black Elk Speaks

Trained as a Lakota holy man, Black Elk became upset by the effect reservation life was having on his people. Government agents outlawed the Lakota's religious ceremonies, such as the Sun Dance. White missionaries also tried to make Indians forget their own religion and become Christians. Black Elk was afraid that soon the Lakota would lose their religious traditions.

To preserve his vast knowledge of Lakota religion, culture, and history for generations to come, Black Elk shared his story with white poet John C. Neihardt during the summer of 1930. Based on their conversations, Neihardt wrote *Black Elk Speaks* (1932), a book long popular with Indians and non-Indians alike. Since its publication, Black Elk's teachings have inspired many Lakota to revive their ancestors' spiritual beliefs.

The Return of the Buffalo

In 1991, on a chilly day in February, leaders from 19 tribes came together in the Black Hills of South Dakota to discuss what they could do to bring back the buffalo. During the meeting, the InterTribal Bison Cooperative was formed. This group helps tribes raise their own buffalo herds, which now include more than 8,000 animals. The growing buffalo population is an important symbol to Plains Indians: They believe, as their ancestors did, that when the buffalo prospers, so will their people.

"The Indians must conform to 'the white man's ways,' peaceably if they will, forcibly if they must."

—Thomas J. Morgan, commissioner of Indian affairs, 1889

What was Wounded Knee II?

In the early 1970s, older traditional Lakota on the Pine Ridge Indian Reservation in South Dakota were being harassed by the reservation's police force. To bring attention to their plight, a group of young activists (calling themselves the American Indian Movement) joined with the elders in 1973 to take over the site of the Wounded Knee Massacre. Living in a trading post and church, hundreds of protesters occupied Wounded Knee for 71 days, as the police and FBI armed with rifles and machine guns swarmed nearby. The bravery and determination of the Wounded Knee activists impressed people throughout the world. For non-Indians, the protest was a lesson in the injustices Indians have suffered throughout history. For Indians, it was an inspiration to fight for Indian rights and work to improve the lives of their people.

AMERICAN INDIANS OF THE SOUTHWEST

Which Indian groups settled in the Southwest?

About 1,700 years ago, ancient Indians of the Hohokam, Mogollon, and Anasazi cultures began establishing farming villages in the Southwest. Many of the Indians who live there today are these early peoples' descendants. The Pueblo Indians of New Mexico were probably descended from the Anasazi, while the Akimel O'odham (also known as the Pima) and the Tohono O'odham (also known as the Papago) of southwestern Arizona are most likely the distant relatives of the Hohokam people. Relative newcomers to the area are the Navajo and the Apache. Both groups came to the Southwest from the North starting in about 1000.

Who are the Pueblo Indians?

The Pueblo Indians are a group of peoples who had lived in the Southwest for almost 1,000 years before non-Indians began arriving in their lands in the mid-sixteenth century. The early Spanish explorers believed that the Pueblo Indians were all members of the same group because they lived in similar houses. They called these houses and the people who lived in them "pueblos," the Spanish word for "village" or "town."

Although they shared a way of life, the Pueblos did not consider themselves one people. Each village, instead, was like an independent nation. Still today, the Pueblo peoples

The word pueblo, which means "town" or "village" in Spanish, is used by non-Indians to describe both the traditional dwellings and the native peoples of the American Southwest who lived in them. However, Pueblo Indians usually identify themselves by the name of their village.

of the Rio Grande Valley in New Mexico usually do not called themselves Pueblos, but rather identify themselves by their village name. The Zuni and Hopi, who live further to the west, are also Pueblo peoples.

What is a pueblo?

A pueblo is the type of house built by the Pueblo peoples. This dwelling was like an apartment building, providing living space for many different families. It had several stories built in tiers so that the roof on one story could be used as a balcony by the people living in the story above.

Keeping the Pueblo Safe

The Pueblo Indians were peaceful peoples who rarely attacked other peoples. But often they did need to fight to protect themselves from Apache, Navajo, and other groups who raided their villages to steal the stores of corn the Pueblo people worked so hard to grow. To keep these invaders out of their homes, they built the entrances to their living areas in the roofs of their pueblos. The entrances were reached by climbing a ladder. If an enemy tried to get inside a pueblo, the inhabitants could merely kick the ladder, a strategy that protected their homes and injured the intruder at the same time.

Precious Water

In her autobiography *Me and Mine* (1969), Helen Sekaquaptewa, who grew up as a traditional Hopi, wrote of what water meant to her people: *"Every drop of water was precious, and there was never enough. From infancy we were taught to drink sparingly; even then, there were times when we were always thirsty. You never asked for a drink when visiting a neighbor's house but went home to drink from your own water....There was concern about the future of the village. Were the water supply to diminish and the population increase, what would become of the people?"*

In pleasant weather, families spent much of their day on these balconies, which had plenty of space for grinding corn, cooking meals, and performing other daily household tasks.

Pueblos were built around a central plaza, where people in the village gathered to perform ceremonies. The houses were constructed from blocks of sandstone plastered with mud or from adobe—bricks of clay and mud that the Pueblo Indians made themselves. Adobe could absorb the heat of the sun, then release it slowly so pueblos stayed comfortable both during hot days and on cold desert nights.

Inside a pueblo were living spaces and storage areas, where dried corn was kept. Each family had its own room, which was sparsely furnished with a few baskets, pots, and blankets that served as chairs during the day and beds at night.

What did the Pueblo Indians farm?

By about 500, early Pueblo Indians had learned how to grow corn from Mesoamerican Indians. The strain of corn they planted was very hearty—it could survive in the dry Southwest. The Pueblo peoples later began growing beans and squash as well.

But even with plants well adapted to their harsh environment, keeping the crops alive was a continual struggle for the Pueblo peoples. They had to invent ways of irrigating their fields to make the most of what little rain they had. But sometimes, even their complex irrigation methods

Many members of southwestern tribes, such as the Quechan and the Mojave, tattooed their chins with dark lines. A tattoo was made by pricking the skin with a cactus needle and rubbing charcoal into the tiny wounds.

were not enough. In a year of drought, their crops would fail and entire villages would go hungry.

What was a kiva?

A kiva was an underground chamber where the Pueblo people held religious ceremonies and their men gathered to socialize. The chamber represented the underworld where they believed human beings once lived. The ladder they used to climb into the chamber symbolized the link between the real world and the underworld.

Who were the kachinas?

Kachinas were spirit beings revered by the Pueblo Indians. There were several hundred kachinas, each with a different name and appearance. They were thought to have the power to make rain. Because rain was needed to grow the crops on which the Pueblo depended, the kachinas had control over their very lives.

To ask the kachinas for help, the Pueblo held ceremonies, during which men dressed up and danced in kachina masks. Decorated with feathers and painted with designs representing rain, lightning, and corn, these masks were thought to be very powerful. The Pueblo believed that when a person placed one over his head, he was transformed into the kachina the mask represented.

What was the Kachinvaki?

The Kachinvaki was the first ceremony attended by a Hopi child. Its purpose was to initiate girls and boys into Hopi society and tell them what would be expected of them as adults.

Children were deemed ready for the Kachinvaki usually sometime between the ages of six and nine. Each was assigned a sponsor, a man or a woman who prepared the child for the ceremony by telling him or her about the kachinas and their power. On the day of the Kachinvaki, the children were taken into a kiva, where they were met by dancers wearing kachina masks. One dancer held a whip made of yucca branches. Told to put their hands above their heads, the children were whipped lightly by the dancer, often with the encouragement of their parents, who told the kachinas about the naughty things their children had done.

The kachina dancers later visited the children at their home and brought them presents. The children were then taken to an all-night dance, where one by one the dancers removed their masks to reveal that they were in fact men. The boys and girls were told not to tell their secret to younger children before they learned the dancers' true identity at their own Kachinvaki ceremony.

To teach children about the kachinas, Pueblo parents gave them wooden dolls painted to represent kachina spirits.

Who were the Koshare?

The Koshare were a group of men who acted like clowns during Pueblo religious ceremonies. With their legs and bodies painted in broad black-and-white stripes, they shouted out jokes, teased onlookers, made fun of sacred rituals, and generally did everything the Pueblo people would normally frown upon.

The Koshare worked hard to entertain their audience, and crowds were free to laugh at them, even when they appeared during otherwise serious ceremonies. Aside from providing comic relief, the Koshare served an important function: By showing how ridiculous and possibly destructive bad behavior could be, they reminded the Pueblo Indians to respect the rules of their society.

When did the Pueblo Indians first encounter non-Indians?

Drawn by rumors of the fabled Seven Cities of Cibola, which were supposedly full of gold, a small group of Spanish explorers led by Marcos de Niza traveled north from Mexico. In 1539 they came upon a group of Zuni, who killed one of the men—de Niza's black slave Estevan—and drove off the rest.

The next year, a larger force led by Francisco de Coronado returned to Zuni territory. They captured a Zuni village near what is now Albuquerque, New Mexico, and explored the area, plundering the villages they came upon. To the relief of the Pueblo Indians, when the Spanish found no gold, they decided to return home. The Pueblo people did not see Spaniards again until nearly 50 years later, when colonists led by Juan de Oñate came to settle permanently in their lands.

How did the Pueblo Indians get along with the Spanish colonists?

The Pueblo peoples were willing to coexist with the newcomers, but the Spanish were not so giving. They angered the Pueblo peoples by trying to force them to become Christians. To discourage the Indians from practicing their own religion, Spanish priests destroyed masks and other ceremonial objects and filled their kivas with sand. They also imprisoned their religious leaders for performing witchcraft. Three Pueblo men convicted of sorcery were hanged in public in 1675.

The Spanish also infuriated the Pueblo people by taking a portion of the Indians' crops. In years of little rainfall, the food demanded by the Spanish was almost all the Pueblo were able to grow. Many people went hungry, and large numbers died from famine or from European diseases introduced by the Spanish. From 1600 to 1680, the Pueblo population dropped from about 50,000 to 17,000.

What was the Pueblo Revolt?

After 80 years of mistreatment, the Pueblo had had enough. Leaders from various villages held secret meetings and decided that they had to drive the Spanish from their lands. Led by a man named Pope, their rebellion began on August 10, 1680. They first told the Spanish to leave and allowed everyone who did to escape with their lives. They then attacked those who remained, killing about 400 people. Once the Spanish were gone, the Pueblo raiders destroyed every object they had left behind and set the priests' mission buildings on fire.

Did the Spanish ever return to Pueblo territory?

Twelve years later, Spanish colonists once again moved onto Pueblo land. With the drop in the population, the Pueblo Indians were so weakened they were not able to fight off the intruders this time. For their part, the Spanish, scared of another rebellion, treated the Indians with a somewhat more even hand.

In time, some Pueblo people accepted that the Spanish were in their territory to stay. They came to live peacefully alongside the intruders and even adopted some elements of their Catholic religion. Others left their lands and moved to areas the Spanish had not invaded. One group of refugees went to the lands of their Hopi relatives to the west and established the village of Hano there. Another joined the Navajo tribe, and still another founded a new pueblo called Laguna.

Do the Pueblo Indians still live in their homelands?

Yes. In 1821, the Spanish surrendered their lands to Mexico, which in turn gave them to the United States in 1848. But no matter which group of non-Indians—Spaniards, Mexicans, or Americans—claimed to have control over the Pueblo, they worked to retain their traditional territory and ways. Because of their perseverance, the Rio Grande Pueblo now occupy 19 separate villages in New Mexico, while the Hopi live on a reservation in Arizona. Not only do the Pueblo peoples of today live in the lands of their ancestors, but they also still observe many of their forebears' religious and cultural customs.

Who are the Diné?

Diné is the name the Navajo call themselves. It means "people" in the Navajo language. Now the largest southwestern tribe, the Navajo's ancestors originally lived farther to the north, possibly in Canada. Starting in about 1000, they moved south, eventually settling near the Pueblo in what is now northwestern New Mexico and northeastern Arizona.

What did the Navajo learn from the Pueblo Indians?

Before the Navajo came to the Southwest, they lived by hunting game and gathering plants. Few wild animals and plants, however, lived in their new hot, dry homeland. To survive, they looked to the Pueblo Indians and learned by their example how to farm corn and squash. Pueblo people who moved to Navajo lands to escape the Spanish also taught the tribe about the ceremonies they performed to ensure a large, healthy harvest. The Navajo began performing their own versions of Pueblo ceremonies, which became a central part of Navajo life.

What was the Blessingway?

The Blessingway was a ceremony held by the Navajo to ensure that a person would live long and well. It was usu- ally performed when a person reached a milestone in his or her life. For instance, a Blessingway might be held to celebrate a marriage, a birth, or a girl's initiation into womanhood.

During the Blessingway, singers told of the beginning of the Navajo world and of the struggles of First Man and First Woman. These legendary figures had a baby named Changing Woman. The Navajo believed that they were created by Changing Woman from shavings of her own skin.

What was hozho?

Hozho was a Navajo word that meant beauty and order. The Navajo believed that in their world, everything

Modern Pueblo Indian potters are world-renowned. Grandmother Joy Navasie and her grandson Charlie are Hopi potters, shown here working at home.

Maria Martinez: Master Potter

Maria Martinez (c. 1887–1980) was a potter from San Ildefonso Pueblo. As a girl, she learned from her aunt how to make clay pottery just as her ancestors had. But Martinez, with her husband, Julian, developed a new way of decorating Pueblo pots. To harden a finished pot, the Pueblo potters fired it by placing it in a bed of hot coals. The Martinezes found that if they placed animal dung on the coals, they could raise a huge cloud of smoke that would blacken a pot's surface. They also discovered that if before firing they painted designs on a pot using a mixture of clay and water, the painted areas would take on a shiny sheen. Using this technique, Martinez was able to create black pots subtly decorated with glossy black patterns. Her unique "black-on-black" pottery style made Maria Martinez famous throughout the world.

was where it should be and, because it was in order, it was beautiful. Through their religious ceremonies and personal behavior, all Navajo strove to maintain hozho.

What were drypaintings?

Drypaintings were sacred images made by the Navajo during ceremonies such as the Blessingway. A holy man used sand, cornmeal, pollen, and pounded roots and barks to create symbols and pictures of spirit-beings on the ground. These images were thought to have great power, so after the ceremony they were always destroyed so they could not harm anyone. Although traditionally drypaintings were meant to be temporary, some Indians artists in the nineteenth century began making permanent versions of them to sell to non-Indians.

What was a hogan?

A hogan was the type of house the Navajo built after they arrived in the Southwest. Hogans were round one-room structures made from a frame of wood poles covered with mud. Each had one entrance, which faced east, and a hole in the roof to release smoke from cooking fires set inside the house.

The Navajo believed that the hogan was a gift to them from Talking God. He told the people not only how to build

Navajo Sheepherding

Traditionally, the Navajo were the most skilled Indian ranchers in the Southwest. In addition to keeping large herds of horses, they raised huge flocks of sheep. (Like horses, these animals were introduced to North America by the Spanish.) Almost every Navajo had a few sheep. Even small children were given lambs to look after so they would know how to care for the animals they would own when they grew up.

Each spring, women and men used knives to shear off the outer layers of their animals' woolly coats. Women then spun the wool into yarn, which they used to weave warm blankets for their families. The Navajo also raised sheep for their meat. A favorite dish was mutton stew, in which chunks of meat from older sheep were combined with cooked vegetables.

Hogan means "home place" in the Navajo language.

these homes, but also how to care for them, since hogans were thought to be alive. When a family built a new hogan, its members gathered to sing special house-blessing songs and sprinkle corn pollen to the north, south, east, and west. By performing these rituals, the family ensured that they would live in harmony within their home.

When did the Navajo first encounter non-Indians?

Expeditions of Spanish soldiers first came to Navajo territory in the late sixteenth century. Although the Navajo sometimes traded with these intruders, more often they fought with them to protect their own territory. This pattern continued in the nineteenth century, when the Navajo lands became first a part of Mexico, then part of the United States. Whenever outsiders tried to push them out of their lands, the Navajo raided and attacked their settlements.

What was the Long Walk?

In the early 1860s, Navajo were stealing cattle and horses from whites in what is now New Mexico. American militiamen, led by Brigadier General James A. Carleton, were sent out to stop them. After a series of bloody battles, the Navajo were defeated and forced to move to a reservation called Bosque Redondo to the east of their homeland.

The tribe's grueling journey there became known as the Long Walk.

The living conditions at Bosque Redondo were terrible. Many people died of starvation and disease. The reservation's arid land was nearly impossible to farm, so the Navajo had to rely on food rations from the U.S. government to survive. Deciding the rations were too expensive, the United States finally allowed the Navajo to return home. After four years at Bosque Redondo, the tribe happily resettled on a 100-square-mile reservation in the heart of its original territory.

What is a Navajo rug?

The Navajo have a long history as weavers. They were introduced to weaving on an upright loom by Pueblo Indians who moved to Navajo territory after fleeing from the Spanish in the mid-seventeenth century. Inspired by designs on Spanish cloth, Navajo weavers soon began using wools colored with vegetable dyes to create brilliant and distinctive geometric patterns.

Traditionally, the Navajo women wove blankets, which their families used as bedding and clothing. Only in the late nineteenth century did they begin to make the rugs for which they are best known today. By that time, white merchants

Friends of the Forty-Niners

In 1848, gold was discovered in California. The next year, thousands of hopeful non-Indian miners, nicknamed Forty-Niners, traveled west to seek their fortunes. The trip was difficult, particularly for those on the southern wagon route that passed through the hottest, driest lands in the Southwest.

Many hungry, thirsty forty-niners found relief in the lands of the Pima (now known as the Akimel O'odham), near present-day Tucson, Arizona. Unlike other Indian groups, such as the Apache, the Pimas welcomed the white travelers. In their desert homeland, they could at best eke out a meager existence. They were, therefore, happy to find forty-niners willing to give them money and goods in exchange for the pumpkins, watermelons, and other foods they grew. While most Indians suffered at the hands of the miners, for a short time the enterprising Pima grew wealthy doing business with them.

According to their legends, the Navajo were taught how to weave by Spider-woman. Parents rubbed spider webs into the hands of baby girls to make sure they would grow up to be skilled weavers.

had set up trading posts in Navajo territory. These business-men bought weavings from the Navajo, then resold them at a profit to non-Indians. The merchants suggested that Navajos make rugs in addition to blankets because rugs could fetch higher prices.

Who were the Navajo Code Talkers?

During World War II, the U.S. Marines were searching for a way they could send top secret messages that their Japanese enemies could not understand. A Navajo engineer, Philip Johnston, suggested that they employ Navajo soldiers as messengers. Using their native language, they could tell each other the sensitive information. Even if the Japanese intercepted a message, Johnston believed they wouldn't be able to interpret the complex Navajo language.

The Marines agreed it was worth a try. They signed up 29 young Navajo men to develop and use a simple code based on their language. Their efforts were so suc-

The Code Talker Alphabet

The Navajo Code Talkers used Navajo words to stand in for English words or phrases. For instance, *de-he-tih-hi* (Navajo for "humming bird") meant "fighter plane" and besh-lo ("iron fish") meant submarine.

The Code Talkers memorized a special alphabet to spell out uncommon English words, like place-names. In this alphabet, a different Navajo word was used to represent each letter.

a	*wol-la-chee*	ant	h	*lin*	horse
b	*shush*	bear	i	*tkin*	ice
c	*moasi*	cat	j	*tkele-cho-gi*	jackass
d	*be*	deer	k	*klizzie-yazzie*	kid
e	*dzeh*	elk	l	*dibeh-yazzie*	lamb
f	*ma-e*	fox	m	*na-as-tso-si*	mouse
g	*klizzie*	goat	n	*nesh-chee*	nut
			o	*ne-ahs-jah*	owl
			p	*bi-so-dih*	pig
			q	*ca-yeilth*	quiver
			r	*gah*	rabbit
			s	*dibeh*	sheep
			t	*than-zie*	turkey
			u	*no-da-ih*	Ute
			v	*a-keh-di-glini*	victor
			w	*gloe-ih*	weasel
			x	*al-an-as-dzoh*	cross
			y	*tsah-as-zih*	yucca
			z	*besh-do-gliz*	zinc

cessful that the Marines eventually recruited more than 400 Navajo Code Talkers. These valiant soldiers are now honored as heroes for helping the United States win its war against Japan.

What is Navajo life like today?

Today, the Navajo are the second-largest tribe in the United States, but they live on the largest reservation. Through many negotiations with the U.S. government, the Navajo have been able to triple the size of the reservation granted to them in 1868. Located in northeastern Arizona and northwestern New Mexico, the Navajo Indian Reservation is now about the same size as the state of West Virginia. The large Navajo Nation is governed by a tribal council that operates programs to improve the education, health, housing, and employment opportunities of the Navajo people.

Pima Indian Ira Hayes was one of six U.S. Marines who bravely raised the American flag at Iwo Jima, an island in the Pacific Ocean, despite ongoing Japanese gunfire. After World War II, Hayes returned home to discrimination and prejudice, despite his heroism.

Tarahumara Footraces

Despite the influences of white farmers, ranchers, and missionaries, the Tarahumara tribe of northern Mexico still live much as their ancestors did. One of the many features of their traditional culture that remains alive is the footrace. During these tests of endurance, participants might run as far as 100 miles over rough, mountainous terrain. Runners often wear belts from which animal claws and small metal objects are strung so that the noise made as the objects clank together will help keep them alert.

In many ways, the lives of today's Navajo are similar to those of whites in the Southwest. Most speak English and live in the same types of houses and work at the same types of jobs as their non-Navajo neighbors. But all the while, they have preserved Navajo ideals, values, and traditions.

When did Indians first live in California? ◆ Why were
here so many California Indians? ◆ What were Calif-
ornia Indian villages like? ◆ How many tribes lived in
California? ◆ What were the largest California tribes?
◆ What plants and animals did California Indians eat?
Did the Indians of California grow crops? ◆ What was
so special about the California Indian baskets? ◆
What type of houses did California Indians build? ◆
When did California Indians first encounter non-
Indians? ◆ How did meeting non-Indians affect
California tribes? ◆ What was a mission? ◆ Why did
missionary priests want Indians to become Christians?

AMERICAN INDIANS OF CALIFORNIA

When did Indians first live in California?

Although some scholars think humans may have lived
in what is now California as early as 48,000 years ago, people definitely lived there by about 8000 B.C. From that time
to the arrival of non-Indians in about A.D. 1550, the Indian
population in California grew to about 300,000. The area
had the highest concentration of Indians anywhere north
of present-day Mexico.

Why were there so many California Indians?

California features many different environments—from
harsh deserts in the south to great, rainy forests in the
north. Nearly every region offered Indians a wide variety of
wild plants and animals for food and for materials to make
clothing, houses, and tools, so many Indian tribes could
flourish there.

What were California Indian villages like?

Most California Indians lived in small villages. They
tended to stay close to their homes. In their rich environment, they could easily get the necessities of life without
traveling far. As a result, many California Indians rarely
encountered people from faraway villages or from other
tribes. In mountainous areas, villages were sometimes so
isolated that people there might pass their entire lives without ever meeting someone from another village.

Colorful brown, red, black, and white Chumush rock paintings on cave walls typically featured people and animals, as well as curious shapes that might represent stars and planets. This 1930 photograph shows part of Painted Cave, near Santa Barbara, California.

How many tribes lived in California?

There were probably more than 100 tribes in California before non-Indians came to the region. In their own minds, however, California Indians probably did not consider themselves part of a tribe. Because their settlements were so isolated, they thought of themselves more as members of a village or of a small group of neighboring

Chumash Rock Art

Throughout their southern California homeland, the Chumash decorated exposed sandstone and cave walls with brilliant paintings. While other tribes made rock paintings, none were as colorful as those of the Chumash. By crushing colored rocks and mixing the powder with animal fat, they made sticky, thick pigments ranging from sharp yellows to burning reds to cool blues. Using a feather or leaf as a brush, they applied these colors to form human- and animal-like figures and odd shapes that possibly represented stars and planets.

The Chumash may have made their colorful paintings merely to celebrate the world around them. But some scholars think that they played a role in the tribe's *toloache* rituals. *Toloache* was a ceremonial drink that made people hallucinate so that they could communicate with their spirit helpers. The shapes and colors of rock paintings may have been meant to inspire *toloache*-drinkers to see fantastic visions.

California Indian Languages

California Indians spoke about 90 languages. But even peoples who used the same one often spoke very different dialects (regional variations in a language). Two villages' dialects could be as different as English and German. These dialects first grew up because villages had fairly little contact with one another. Once they were well established, these differences in language helped to keep these peoples apart.

villages (sometimes called a tribelet) than as members of a tribe. All people in a small California Indian village were generally treated as equals. Each village or tribelet had a leader, but this person had little real power.

One notable exception was the Chumash, who lived on a 250-mile stretch along the coast of the Pacific Ocean. In large plank boats, the Chumash frequently traveled from village to village to trade or see relatives. This constant contact made the Chumash people far more unified than most California tribes.

What were the largest California tribes?

Many tribes lived in central California between the great mountains of the Sierra Nevada range and the Pacific Ocean. The homelands of the Pomo, Salinan, and Chumash were along the coast, while those of the Yokut, Miwok, and Nisenan were further inland.

Large groups in southern California included the Cahuilla, Gabrielino, Luiseño, and Tipai. They shared many customs and cultural traits with Indians of the American Southwest, such as the Pueblo Indians.

In the Northwest, tribes such as the Hupa, Karok, and Yurok lived in a rainy climate among rich forest lands. Their way of life resembled that of the northwestern Indians in what is now Oregon and Washington more than that of other California peoples.

What plants and animals did California Indians eat?

California Indians could gather wild seeds, plums, grapes, berries, and roots; fish for trout and salmon; and

Building with Tule

In the marshes of northern California, Indians found the ideal material for house-building—a bulrush known as tule. They wove the stalks of this wild plant into large, flexible mats that, placed over a frame of saplings, created the walls of their houses. Airy and light, tule mats kept the Indians' houses cool and comfortable by blocking out harsh sun while letting air flow through.

Roasted grasshopper was a favorite food of Indians in central California.

hunt small birds and game such as rabbits and quail or large herds of elk and deer.

Their most important food, though, was acorns. Wherever great California oak trees grew, fall was the season of the acorn harvest. As soon as the acorns were ripe, boys and young men climbed the oaks and jiggled the branches to shake the nuts loose. When they fell to the ground, women, children, and older people picked them up and placed them in baskets strapped to their backs. At home, the nuts were pounded into a flour, then baked into bread or mixed with water and flavored with berries to make a tasty mush.

Did the Indians of California grow crops?

With some 500 wild plants available to them, the Indians of California generally did not need to bother with the hard work of farming. They did, however, develop many clever ways of helping wild plants grow and flourish.

For instance, at a young age, women in central California learned to keep meadows of wild hyacinths in bloom. Hyacinth plants produce beautiful pink, purple, and white flowers, but, more important to the Indians, their bulbs could be baked and eaten. As women gathered the large edible bulbs, they peeled away small bulb growths and replanted them. They also used sticks to break up the soil, so the new plants could get the air and water they needed. Through the women's careful tending, the hyacinths continued to blossom year after year.

The only crop farmed by most California Indians was tobacco, which they smoked during religious ceremonies.

What type of houses did California Indians build?

Each climate in California called for a different type of house. In the rainy northwest, families constructed large houses out of cedar planks to keep themselves dry. In the moderate north and central California, people spent the winter in pit houses, which they built by digging a round hole in the ground and roofing it with a cone-shaped frame of wooden poles. In the hot south, Indians needed nothing more than simple shelters made of grass or branches to give them some shade from sun.

What type of clothing and tools did they make?

In most of California, the weather was so mild that Indians needed little clothing. Men usually wore a simple thong made of animal skin or nothing at all. Women generally strapped mats woven from strips of bark around their waists.

The tools California Indians made were equally simple. Because plants and animals were so plentiful, they needed only the most basic implements to do the work of food-gathering. For instance, women used sticks carved to a point at one end to dig roots and bulbs from the ground. Women did use great skill and care, however, in crafting one type of object—their baskets.

What was so special about the California Indians' baskets?

Because they relied on wild plants for so much of their diet, California Indians had to know how to make light, strong, and durable blankets. When gathering nuts, berries, and roots, women carried large, cone-shaped baskets fitted with shoulder straps. They used larger baskets to hold the foods they gathered, particularly acorns, which, if properly stored, could stay fresh for a full year. Some tribes also placed acorn meal in small shallow baskets, then tapped the sides to sift large chunks from the fine flour.

To make baskets in all the shapes and sizes they needed, women had to become expert weavers. They took pride in decorating their works by weaving grasses colored with vegetable dyes to create detailed shapes and patterns.

Some California basket-makers wove "baby baskets" to hold their infants while they worked.

These two baskets woven by Pomo Indians in the 1890s are just four and five inches wide. Their small size and intricate patterns display the weaver's skill.

Some groups also added feathers, beads, and other ornaments.

Today the Pomo are particularly well known for their beautiful basketry. To show off their talents, Pomo basketweavers often make spectacular miniature baskets, some as small as a thumbnail.

When did California Indians first encounter non-Indians?

On October 10, 1542, a group of Spanish explorers led by Juan Cabrillo arrived in the lands of the Chumash near what is now the city of Santa Barbara. The Chumash were friendly to the Spaniards, but the Europeans soon left when they did not find the gold they were looking for. Although a few Spanish expeditions visited coastal areas, the Spanish did not settle in California until more than two centuries later, when Spanish priests began to found missions there.

How did meeting non-Indians affect California tribes?

The most important—and most devastating—effect was the Indians' exposure to European diseases, such as measles, cholera, and smallpox. These diseases killed Indians throughout North America, but they were especially deadly in California. Because people lived close together in clusters of villages, disease spread very quickly. Some villages lost as much as 90 percent of their population in a matter of years.

What was a mission?

A mission was a complex of buildings that housed Spanish priests of a particular Catholic order. These priests came to California to convert Indians to Christianity. The missions included quarters for new converts, which the priests called neophytes. The neophytes were expected to live and work at the mission while the priests schooled them in their new religion and taught them about European ways and values. Between 1769 and 1834, 21 missions were built in California.

Artist Ferdinand Deppe painted this picture of San Gabriel Mission in 1832. The Spanish mission architecture is very different from the small thatched Indian home at the right.

Non-Indians named some California tribes after the missions they were associated with. For instance, the Gabrielino's name came from the San Gabriel Mission and the Luiseño's came from the San Luis Rey Mission.

Why did missionary priests want Indians to become Christians?

The Spanish priests believed they were saving the Indians' souls by converting them to Catholicism. They did not think they were interfering with the Indians' religious life because they thought the Indians had no real religion of their own.

In fact, California Indians had a complicated set of religious beliefs. To pay proper respect to nature, they performed a wide variety of dances and rituals. The Hupa of northern California, for example, devoted ten days every fall to the White Deerskin Dance. The Hupa believed that deer would return each hunting season only if this ceremony had been performed properly.

The Indians' religious leaders were also healers. These medicine men and women had a great deal of influence in their villages. If the head of a village could not resolve a dispute, he often turned to a medicine person for help. In part because of medicine peoples' role as peacemakers, California Indians almost never went to war with each other.

Why did Indians go to live in missions?

A few Indians from the villages hardest hit by disease were so desperate and distraught that they welcomed the food and shelter offered by mission priests. Most Indians, however, wanted nothing to do with the missions and the Spanish. They came to the missions only after they were rounded up at gunpoint by Spanish soldiers. Once confined there, they were forced to give up their own religion and work as farmers or tradespeople. If they disobeyed the Spanish, they were whipped or beaten. These punishments, along with starvation and disease spread by bad sanitation, led to the deaths of thousands of mission Indians.

When did the mission system end?

In 1821, Spain lost control of California to Mexico. Thirteen years later, the Mexican government outlawed Indian slavery and allowed the 15,000 Indians living in missions to leave. Many cheered when they were told that they were at last free. But sadly they were unable to go back to their old ways of life. Their villages were destroyed, and Mexicans had taken over much of their lands. With

Toypurina's Rebellion

During the mission period (1769–1834), Indians often banded together to rebel against the Spanish. In 1785, one such uprising was organized by a Gabrielino medicine woman named Toypurina. Under her leadership, six villages of Indians tried to overthrow the priests and soldiers at the San Gabriel Mission near present-day Los Angeles. Toypurina's followers believed that her super-natural powers would lead them to victory, but, warned about the attack, Spanish forces quickly squelched the rebellion and arrested Toypurina.

At her trial, Toypurina bravely spoke out against her people's ill treatment by the Spanish. As a punishment, she was sent to the San Carlos Mission (near what is now Carmel, California) to live out her days in exile from her people.

nowhere else to go, most settled on *rancherías*, huge farms where they lived and worked for wealthy Mexicans.

How did California become part of the United States?

Beginning in 1846, the United States went to war with Mexico over control of lands in what are now California, Texas, and New Mexico. The Americans won the Mexican War (1846–1848), and, in the peace treaty, the United States was given this territory.

Almost immediately, non-Indian Americans flooded into the lands of the California Indians. Some of the Americans were settlers, attracted by the rich lands and pleasant climate. Others were miners, who flocked to California hoping to strike it rich in the Gold Rush.

What was the Gold Rush?

On January 24, 1848, gold was discovered at Sutter's Fort, a ranch and trading center near Culloma, a Nisenan Indian village. Although the ranch's owner tried to keep the discovery secret, word of the gold spread quickly, first in the West and then throughout the East. Hoping to find their own fortune, thousands and thousands of Americans rushed to California to mine for the precious metal during the next three years.

Did California Indians prospect for gold?

Some white prospectors hired Indians to look for gold for them. But most native Californians had little interest in gold, which to them was just a shiny metal. The Gold Rush had its greatest effect on the Indians by bringing ever increasing numbers of non-Indians into their midst. Some of the miners were rough, violent men who killed Indians in their way with little thought. The government of California contributed to the violence by funding military campaigns against Indians. Between 1845 and 1870, as many as 48,000 Indian men, women, and children in the state were murdered.

Most of the survivors saw their lands overrun by settlers and by miners who, giving up the quest for gold, decided to stay in California rather than return home. These newcomers forced many Indian groups to abandon their villages, leaving these peoples landless.

What happened to California's landless tribes?

In the late nineteenth century, a few reservations were established for the many California peoples driven off their land. Life at these reservations was difficult, so poor and homeless Indians began looking to relatives for help. Even though their old villages no longer existed, the ties that bound people together still survived.

Other Indians tried to maintain their traditional ways by hiding in mountain foothills. There they built new communities where they could live as they chose without being threatened by whites.

Who was Ishi?

In August 1911, a group of non-Indians came upon a thin and tired Indian man as he tentatively emerged from the foothills of Mount Lassen in northern California. He was the last surviving member of the Yahi tribe, most of whom had been killed either by non-Indians or the diseases they carried.

When anthropologist Alfred Kroeber heard the story, he arranged for the Yahi man to come to live at the University of California's museum in San Francisco. There, he was named Ishi, the Yahi word for man. Many researchers visited Ishi to ask him questions about Yahi culture.

Through contact with these non-Indians, Ishi was exposed to tuberculosis, a lung disease that killed him in 1916. Although Ishi's death marked the end of the Yahi, knowledge of his people and their ways lived on through the information he shared.

Do Indians still live in California?

In the early twentieth century, the Indian population in California was dwindling away. By 1910, there were only 25,000 Indians left in the state. In the middle of the twentieth century, however, the number began to rise. By 1990, California had an Indian population of about 242,000.

Why did California's Indian population grow so much in the twentieth century?

Probably some of the increase was an illusion. The earlier polls likely underestimated the actual number of Indians in California. In the early decades of the century, people were reluctant to say to pollsters that they were Indians because they were afraid of being treated badly by whites.

But in the 1950s and 1960s, California's Indian population got at least a boost from the U.S. government's relocation program. Relocation was a plan to encourage Indians to move from reservations to cities. The government told Indians that as city-dwellers they could find better jobs and a more comfortable life. But the United States also wanted Indians to relocate so it could save some of the money it spent on operating reservations. Because of the relocation program, Indians from many other states came to live in California's largest cities, particularly San Francisco and Los Angeles.

What was the Alcatraz takeover?

By the late 1960s, young California Indians (many from relocated families) began to speak out against the U.S. government's policies toward Indian peoples. Their most dramatic protest was the Alcatraz takeover.

Alcatraz is a small island in the Pacific Ocean just off the coast of San Francisco, California. For decades, it was the home of a famous federal prison. By the late 1960s,

Alcatraz was still owned by the U.S. government, but the island and the prison were abandoned.

On November 20, 1968, 78 Indians traveled by boat to Alcatraz and illegally set up a camp there. Calling themselves the Indians of All Tribes, they took control of the island, not because they wanted to live there, but because they wanted the attention of politicians and reporters. As police gathered to figure out how to force the protesters to leave Alcatraz, the activists took the opportunity to tell reporters about the problems facing Indians in cities and on reservations—issues reporters usually ignored.

The activists stayed on Alcatraz for 19 months. During that time, their words and concerns were broadcast on television and reported in newspapers throughout the world.

AMERICAN INDIANS OF THE NORTHWEST

Which Indian groups lived in the Northwest?

The Northwest Indians lived in many villages in the lush lands along the Pacific Ocean. This area included the homelands of the Chinook, Makah, and Nootka, who lived along the coasts of what are now the states of Oregon and Washington, and the territory of the Coast Salish tribes, who also lived on the shores of Puget Sound near what is now Seattle, Washington. On the northern Pacific Coast were the Kwakiutl, Bella Bella, and Haida of the present-day Canadian province of British Columbia and the Tlingit of what is now southeastern Alaska.

What kind of environment was the Northwest?

The Indians of the Northwest Coast lived in one of the most comfortable environments in North America. The winters were never very cold, and the summers were never hot. Although it rained many months of the year, the damp weather allowed plants and great forests to flourish. From cedar trees, Indians could make almost everything they needed to live. The cedar gave them the wood they used to build their houses, but even more important was the tree's bark. Cedar bark, cut into thin, flexible strips, could be woven into baskets, fishing nets, mats, and even clothing.

What foods did the Northwest Indians eat?

Some Northwest Indians hunted deer and elk or gathered wild fruits and berries. But by far, most of their food

On stormy nights, Coast Salish parents sometimes woke up their children, gave them an icy bath, and sent them outside to run through the rain. The Indians believed this practice made girls and boys grow up strong and healthy.

came from the ocean and rivers, which were brimming with fish and other sea life. Indians to the south, such as the Chinook, could make an excellent meal merely by walking along the beach and picking up clams, mussels, and oysters that washed ashore. Sometimes a dead whale was swept onto a beach. An entire village would then come together to skin the whale and share the delicious meat. In a few northern groups, such as the Makah and Nootka, men sought prestige among their people by canoeing into the rough Pacific waters and hunting whales with hand-thrown spears.

Fish, however, made up the greatest part of the Indians' seafood diet. Area waters offered them herring, halibut, and, most important, five species of salmon. To catch fish, Northwest Indians developed a wide array of hooks, nets, spears, harpoons, and other fishing tools. Some groups even used fishing rakes that could pierce smaller fish as they were pulled along through the water.

Why were salmon so important to northwestern Indians?

The rivers of the Northwest were full of salmon that were easy to catch as they made their annual swim upriver to lay their eggs. In the spring, as the salmon runs began, entire villages left their homes to set up camp along the rivers' edge. Using large nets woven from strips of cedar bark, fishermen could scoop up huge numbers of fish as they swam by. They also used traps, called weirs, to force the salmon to swim right into their nets.

The Nootka Whale House

Successful whale hunters were highly respected by the Nootka Indians. To honor them, they built a special shrine, now known as the Whale House. The Nootka Whale House contained wooden whale carvings, human skulls, and carved figures of whalers who had died. Medicine men performed ceremonies in the house so that more dead whales would wash up on the shore.

Indians living along the Pacific Coast got most of their food from the ocean and rivers. Here, villagers work together to skin a dead whale, which provided meat for food and oil to burn for heat and light.

Once the fish were caught, women did the work of preserving them so salmon could be eaten year-round. In drier climates, the fish were hung on strings or set on racks and left outside to dry in the sun. In rainy areas, they were placed in smokehouses, where the smoke from a large fire dried out the fish. Women were able to store and preserve so many fish that their families could eat nothing but salmon and never go hungry.

What was a First Salmon Ceremony?

At the beginning of the salmons' annual run, Northwest fishermen performed a ritual after they caught the first fish. During the ceremony, the fish was roasted and eaten, usually with a small bite given to each person in a village. The bones were then returned to the river in which the salmon was caught.

The Indians believed that salmon chose to give up their lives so that people could live. Through the First

Northwest Indians believed that salmon were humans who came to earth in fish form. The five species of Northwest salmon were thought to live as five different tribes.

Oily and Delicious

One of the greatest delicacies of the Northwest Indian diet was the oil of the tiny eulachon fish. Indian fishermen placed their eulachon catch in large covered pits for several days. They then boiled the fish and scooped up the oil that collected on the surface. Used to season dried fish, fruits, and berries, the oil was stored in special wooden bowls that were often carved with beautiful designs. Some bowls, now in museums, were so saturated that they still ooze oil even though they have not been used for more than 100 years.

Eulachon were also known as candlefish because Indians used these oily fish as torches. Once lit, a dried eulachon could burn like a candle for hours.

Salmon Ceremony, fishermen showed their gratitude for the salmon's sacrifice. Only by demonstrating their respect for the fish could the fishermen be sure that the salmon would return the next year.

What type of houses did Northwest Indians build?

In the Northwest, great forests of cedar trees provided Indians with an ideal building material. The trunks of these trees could be easily split into planks as long as 40 feet. Using these planks, Indians built large, sturdy wooden houses that were well suited to their rainy climate. Plank houses were clustered to form villages, which were usually located along the beach. The entrance to a plank house normally faced the ocean.

To the Northwest Indians, a plank house was more than just a place to live. It was a symbol of a family's social position. Most of the Indians' wealth belonged to just a few families, who had the greatest power in their villages. An important family's house was painted with designs of animals and other creatures. Along with totem poles, these paintings were emblems of a family's privileged place in society.

What was a totem pole?

A totem pole was a giant sculpture carved from the trunk of a cedar tree. Wealthy families hired artists to create totem poles, which they proudly placed outside their houses. By displaying a totem pole, a family could let everyone in the village know how important and powerful it was.

The carvings on a totem pole were carefully chosen to tell a story. Through images of humans, animal, and beings from the spirit-world, they depicted moments in the family's history. Usually they told of how supernatural beings gave the family spiritual power. Claiming this type of special relationship with spirits allowed a rich family to say it deserved all the privileges its wealth could buy. To keep this close connection to the spirit-world alive, a totem pole owner might place food or tobacco in front of the pole as a gift to the spirit-beings.

How were totem poles made?

Originally, totem poles were carved using bone tools. These were difficult to use, so traditional carvings were fairly simple. But when non-Indians came to the Northwest, they gave Indians metal tools that sliced through cedar smoothly and easily. These tools freed artists to create more and more elaborate figures. They used them to dig out the faces of thunderbirds, whales,

Erected outside a family's house, each totem pole told the story of that family through carefully selected images. These poles were erected in a Haida village near Howkan, Alaska.

The Coast Salish bred special small woolly dogs. Each spring, they shaved the dogs' hair, spun it into yarn, and used it to weave warm woolly blankets.

grizzly bears, ravens, and other creatures, one on top of each other, until the entire pole was covered. The artist then painted the carvings using dyes made from vegetables. The most popular colors were red, black, and white.

Erecting a finished totem pole was hard work and sometimes involved hundreds of people. First, the crowd dug a deep pit into the ground where the bottom of the pole would sit. Next, they tied ropes to the top of the pole as it lay on the ground. After moving the pole's bottom next to the pit, they slowly pulled on the ropes until the pole stood upright. They then stuffed the pit tight with rocks and dirt until the totem pole was held firmly in place.

Metal objects called coppers, usually engraved with an image of an animal, were symbols of wealth and status in Northwest Indian culture. Tutlthidi, a chief, here gives away a copper to fellow villagers in honor of his son.

Head-Flattening

Among many Northwest Indians, the most attractive feature a person could have was a sloped forehead. To ensure their children would be beautiful, they strapped their babies into a bed called a cradle board that had a piece of wood hinged to the top. The wood applied a gentle pressure to a baby's soft skull. After about a year in a cradle board, the front of a baby's skull flattened into the shape the Indians' admired. Although disturbing to the non-Indians who visited the tribe, the process, known as head-flattening, was painless and had no effect on a baby's intelligence.

What was a potlatch?

In many Northwest Indian groups, prominent families held great feasts called potlatches. In addition to food, guests enjoyed singing and dancing. They were also treated to giveaways, in which the host family offered gifts to everyone who attended. Traditionally, gifts included blankets, food, wool robes, canoes, and even slaves. Yet, the most extravagant gift a potlatch guest could receive was a piece of a copper.

The word potlatch meant "to give" in the Nootka Indian language.

What was a copper?

A copper was a flat, shieldlike object made out of copper metal that the Indians obtained through trade with whites. Owned by chiefs, they were usually engraved with an image of an animal that was thought to have a special spiritual connection with the owner's family.

Coppers were treasured because families believed they held the souls of their ancestors. They were also symbols of wealth and status: By owning a copper, people reminded their village that they had a high social rank. Coppers could be very expensive to buy. In the nineteenth century, for instance, one copper was sold for 10,000 blankets.

Why would an Indian family hold a potlatch?

Potlatches were usually held to announce that a new person was taking the position of chief. Some Indian

Every copper had a name. For example, a particularly valuable one was called "All Other Coppers Are Ashamed to Look at It." Another was named "Causing Destruction" because two people who owned it were murdered.

groups, however, used them to celebrate more personal events, such as a marriage or the naming of a child. Occasionally, a chief might hold a small potlatch if he had been embarrassed in public. For instance, if he fell out of a canoe in front the village, he might distribute gifts as a way of buying back his dignity.

No matter what the occasion, a host family had another reason for holding a potlatch. In Northwest Indian cultures, people's place in society was not determined by how much wealth they kept, but how much they were willing and able to give away. To maintain the respect of other people in their village, a wealthy family had to host a potlatch from time to time.

Winter ceremonials featured spirited dances that relayed stories of the supernatural. Noted photographer Edward Curtis immortalized this dramatic moment in the Hamatsa Dance, depicting the Cannibal emerging from the woods.

Often, families used potlatches to compete with one another for social status. Among the Kwakiutl in the early twentieth century, an elaborate potlatch could cost a family as much as $40,000. In addition to traditional goods, give-aways at these events might include manufactured items such as sewing machines, pool tables, and outboard motors.

What were Winter Ceremonials?

In the spring and summer, most Northwest Indians could catch and preserve enough fish to feed them throughout the rest of the year. This left groups such as the Kwakiutl, Bella Bella, and the Tsimshian free to devote winter months to staging elaborate ceremonies. Through these ceremonies, the Indians performed dances that told stories about the supernatural beings they believed controlled the universe.

Winter ceremonials were staged to create high drama and often made use of special effects that rival modern theater productions. Menacing ghost spirits that seemed to dance without human assistance were in fact marionettes, their strings invisible in the soft, ceremonial light. The eyes of the evil, child-eating Dzonkwa, which seemed to pop

Canoe Burial

Many Indians living along the Pacific Coast showed respect to their most honored dead by burying them in canoes. For instance, when a Tillamook chief died, his followers thoroughly washed the body, painted his face red, and wrapped him in a blanket held tight with strips of cedar bark. The body was then placed on a bed in a deserted house and visited for several days by mourners, who struggled not to fall asleep in the presence of the body for fear the chief would take them with him to the land of the dead.

Then, the corpse was moved to the burial ground in the early morning, when mourners believed the other buried souls would be asleep. At last, the chief's body was placed in its final home—a richly decorated canoe held above the ground on posts. A second, smaller canoe was put upside down over the corpse, while mourners hung grave offerings from the canoe with rope. If the chief's family were very wealthy, a year later they might have another burial ceremony, during which the body would be uncovered, re-washed, and then reburied.

out of her face, were actually sheep eyes that before the ceremony had been planted in the hair of the dancer depicting her. And one spirit-creature suddenly appeared to turn into another with the help of brilliantly designed "transformation masks," whose moving parts allowed dancers to reveal one mask hidden behind another.

Who was the Cannibal-at-the-North-End-of-the-World?

Among the Kwakiutl Indians, the most important ritual of the winter ceremonials was a dance performed by a special group known as the Hamatsa Society. The Hamatsa Dance told the story of their ancestor, the Cannibal-at-the-North-End-of-the-World—a powerful spiritual being who was said to feed on human flesh.

The Hamatsa Dance was performed by a young Kwakiutl who was being initiated into the society. He was accompanied by several performers wearing huge wooden masks over their heads to depict Raven, Cannibal's helper. During the dance, as the initiate was overtaken by the Cannibal's spirit, he began to flail around wildly. The dancer sometimes ran into the audience and started biting the arms of spectators. (Before the ceremonies, these audience members usually agreed to be bitten in exchange for a gift.) Also on hand were the Fool Dancers. They kept an eye on the audience and threw rocks at anyone who did not behave properly. At the end of the Hamatsa Dance, the initiate was tamed as the Cannibal's spirit was driven from his body.

When did Northwest Indians first meet non-Indians?

In the late eighteenth century, non-Indians from Europe and Russia began to travel the sea to the Northwest Coast. The first were explorers, but soon they were followed by traders. These businessmen sailed from Spain, Russia, and England to participate in the Maritime Fur Trade.

What was the Maritime Fur Trade?

The Maritime Fur Trade refers to a trade network that developed between Northwest Indians and foreign non-

Indian traders. The non-Indians wanted seal furs, which they could resell in China for an enormous profit. In exchange for seal furs, Indian traders received guns, woven cloth, and European metals, especially copper and iron. They also liked to bargain for Chinese coins, which they used to decorate their own clothing.

Northwest Indians almost always had the upper hand in the Maritime Fur Trade. They did not have to have the goods the non-Indian traders offered, but the non-Indian traders, after traveling across the globe, needed to fill their ships with seal furs or they would lose all the money they spent on the trip. The Indians took full advantage of the situation. They learned to drive a hard bargain and refused to trade with anyone whose goods were not of the highest quality. One French trader who dealt with the Tlingit claimed that they "bargained with as much skill as any tradesman in Europe."

What was Chinook Jargon?

The Maritime Fur Trade brought together traders from Russia, England, France, and many Indian nations. To make deals, they had to be able to negotiate with one another, but nobody knew everyone else's language. So that they could speak with one another, at least enough to trade, they developed a special language called Chinook Jargon. It took words from English, French, and several Indian languages, including Chinook, Nootka, and Salish, and combined them to make new words and phrases. Anyone who spoke one of these languages could learn Chinook Jargon quickly and easily. Although Chinook Jargon speakers could not communicate complicated ideas, the simple language allowed many different peoples to do business together.

Who were Lewis and Clark?

In 1803, President Thomas Jefferson bought the Louisiana Purchase, a huge area of land between the Mississippi River and the Rocky Mountains in the center of what is now the United States. To find out more about the region and the people who lived there, he sent out a small

Deal-Making—Chinook Style

Some Indian groups grew wealthy by acting as middlemen. The Chinook, for instance, who lived along the Pacific Coast near the mouth of the Columbia River, were the first Indians to meet trading ships that sailed into the region. The Chinook soon found that they could make a big profit by traveling inland, buying furs from Indians there at a low price, then going home and reselling to non-Indian traders at a far higher price.

To retain their privileged position, the Chinook did everything they could to keep other Indians from dealing directly with the foreign traders. They told the inland tribes that the whites were cannibals who wanted to eat them. When the Chinook bought guns from non-Indians they went even further: When inland tribes offered them furs at prices they did not like, the Chinook took to shooting guns in the air. The inland tribes, who had no guns, got the point. Shaken, they offered their furs to the Chinook at whatever price they wanted.

team of explorers led by Meriwether Lewis and William Clark.

In the fall of 1805, the Lewis and Clark expedition reached the Pacific Ocean. There, they were met by the Chinook and the Clatsop, who lived along the mouth of the Columbia River. Accustomed to trading with whites, the Indians were friendly to the visitors and became their trading partners. The Clatsop persuaded the explorers to spend the winter in their lands, where Lewis and Clark built a cluster of cabins they called Fort Clatsop.

Was contact with non-Indians good for Northwest Indians?

At first, Indians welcomed non-Indians into their lands. They liked the new goods traders offered, and traders, eager just to do business, did not try to hurt them, change their ways, or take their lands.

By the early 1800s, however, the situation began to change. The fur trade fell on hard times because Indians had killed so many seals that few were left to hunt. Indian villages also began suffering from new diseases, such as smallpox, that were introduced to them by the foreign traders. Waves of epidemics killed many Indians. Among the Chinook, for instance, the number of tribe members dropped by half between 1805 and 1851.

Beginning in the 1830s, the Indians in present-day Oregon and Washington also faced a new threat: American settlers. The settlers wanted to take control of these Indians' land because the fertile coastal region made excellent farmland.

What happened to the Indians of Washington?

In 1853, Washington became a territory of the United States. The new territorial governor, Isaac Stevens, was charged with making treaties with all the state's Indians. In the treaties, the Indians were supposed to agree to surrender their land and move to small reservations.

In 1855, Stevens met with many Indian groups and negotiated several treaties. The treaties, though, were hastily

Some Words and Phrases Jargon in Chinook

tupso kopa latate meant hair
tupso – grass (Chinook)
kopa – on (Chinook)
latate – the head (mispronunciation of the French words *la tête*)

cly tumtum meant to mourn
cly – cry (mispronunciation of English)
tumtum – heart (invented word mimicking the sound of a heartbeat)

kah cole chako meant the north
kah – where (Chinook)
cole – cold (mispronunciation of English)
chako – is (Nootka)

saghalie tyee yaka book meant the Bible
saghalie – heaven (Chinook)
tyee – chief (Nootka)
yaka – his (Chinook)
book – book (English)

man yaka delate kumtux potlatch wawa meant orator
man – man (English)
yaka – who (Chinook)
delate – definitely (mispronunciation of the English word *straight*)
kumtux – knows (Nootka)
potlatch – [how to] give (Nootka)
wawa – a speech (Chinook)

Sacagawea

The explorers of the Lewis and Clark expedition owed a great debt to a Shoshone woman named Sacagawea. She and her husband were hired to join the group as interpreters, but Sacagawea did much more to make the expedition a success. When the explorers were low on food, she knew where to find and how to cook wild roots and berries. The foods she gathered were often the only thing that kept the party from starving. She also persuaded her Shoshone relatives to help the explorers cross the Rocky Mountains. Without advice and supplies from the Shoshone, the expedition may not have survived this difficult part of the journey. In appreciation, expedition leader Meriwether Lewis named a river in Montana after Sacagawea. More recently, the United States has honored Sacagawea by featuring her image on a one-dollar coin, to be issued in the year 2000.

put together. Many Indians who signed them probably did not know what they were agreeing to. Some of the treaties also were not ratified by the U.S. Congress. As a result, the Indians who gave up their lands were not given the reservations they were promised. Because the United States was not keeping its part of the deal, in later conferences Indians refused to deal with Stevens at all.

The Stevens treaties were a disaster for the Washington Indians. Many who signed them never received reservations. Others who walked out of the treaty negotiations were also left landless.

What are treaty fishing rights?

In the treaties negotiated with Washington Indians in 1855, the Indians were guaranteed the right to fish in their "usual and accustomed places." Dependent on fish for their survival, the Indians kept fishing at their favorite sites. But as more non-Indians moved into their territory, they tried to force Indian fishermen off prime fishing areas.

In the twentieth century, the Indians decided to exert their rights in a new way—in the courts. After a long legal battle, a 1974 court ruling called the Boldt decision declared that the Indians' treaties gave them rights to half of all the fish in area waters. While this finding was a great

Chief Seattle was photograhed in 1865 holding a basketry rain hat in his lap. The Suquamish leader eloquently defended tribal lands and traditions during the negotiation of the Treaty of Point Elliot in 1855.

victory for the Indians, they still have to fight non-Indian fishermen to give them access to fishing sites and their fair share of the state's fish catch.

A Whaling Tradition Reborn

Throughout most of their history, the Makah were great whale hunters. That tradition came to an end in 1926, when the International Whaling Commission banned whaling in the region. Non-Indian hunters had killed so many whales that the commission feared the whales would die out completely unless all hunting stopped.

With the ban, the whale population increased. By 1996 it had grown so large that the commission approved the Makah's request to revive their whaling tradition. Now with permission to hunt five California gray whales a year, young Makah are relearning the ancient art of whale hunting.

Vhat is the Subarctic? ◆ Which Indians lived in the Subarctic? ◆ How did these Indians live in the cold winter? ◆ Wh... ...Ar...ti... ...he... the Inuit? ◆ How did the Inuit survive in the Arctic? ◆ Aside from meat, what did h... ti... p... ...he... nuit? ◆ How did he Inuit hunt th... prey? ◆ Who was Sedna? ◆ How did the In... travel over the ice? ◆ Did all Inuit live in gloos? ◆ H... ...li... ...ur... ...ed t... ...b... winter? ◆ What was a song duel? ◆ When did non-Indians arrive n the A...ti... ...t w... ...e... ...rive... ...ssage? ◆ How did trading change native life? ◆ When did Sub- ...rctic Indians encounter whites? ◆ Who were the

NATIVES OF THE SUBARCTIC AND ARCTIC

What is the Subarctic?

The Subarctic is a huge area directly below the Arctic Circle that stretches over most of central Canada and Alaska. The land is covered by evergreen forests and great lakes and rivers. In the short Subarctic summer, the air is warm but filled with mosquitoes and flies that hatch by the millions as soon as the temperature rises. In the long winter, the ground is blanketed by snow and the temperature rarely rises above freezing.

Which Indians lived in the Subarctic?

The Innu (also known as the Montagnais-Naskapi) and Beothuk lived in what is now eastern Canada, while present-day central Canada was the home of the Cree and Chipewyan. Farther west were the Beaver and Slavey of present-day western Canada and the Gwich'in and Ingalik of what is now Alaska.

How did these Indians live in the cold winter?

Because it was too cold to farm, Subarctic Indians spent the winter following herds of caribou and moose. Aside from being their main source of food, these animals provided the Indians with skins, from which they made clothes and houses, and bones, which they crafted into tools and weapons.

During the long, harsh winters, Subarctic Indians traveled in small bands hunting for caribou. They carried tents of wood covered in hides, were easy to set up and transport.

When hunting, people usually traveled in small groups made up of only a few families. Each group was led by a skilled hunter, who determined when and where the band should move their camp. Like Plains Indians, Subarctic Indians on the hunt lived in portable cone-shaped tents made from wood and hides that people could put up and take down quickly and easily.

Indians in the Subarctic made snowshoes of all shapes and sizes to help them walk through the deep snows. According to Chipewyan legend, snowshoes were invented by the first man and woman on earth.

How did hunters ensure a good catch?

Subarctic Indians believed that animals would give their lives to humans only if people showed them respect. Different tribes had different rules about how to treat animals properly. The Gwich'in believed that a hunter would insult the animal spirit-world if he counted the animals he killed. Among the Cree, a hunter had to present an animal he had killed to the old people in his band before slaughtering it. He also placed the skulls and antlers of dead moose in a tree, with the skull facing the east so that the

The Fearsome *Windigos*

A hunter's greatest fear was that he might encounter a *windigo*. The Subarctic Indians believed that *windigos* were great giants who stalked through the forests, using treetops as snowshoes. Filthy and vicious, *windigos* had hearts made of ice and great evil powers, including the ability to turn people into cannibals. Hunters, alone and frightened in the frozen wilderness, often reported *windigo* sightings and warned others to avoid the places where these wicked giants had been seen.

dead animal could watch the sunrise. Many Indian groups considered it wrong to speak badly of animals and cautioned children never to laugh at them.

What was the Shaking Tent Ceremony?

When Subarctic Indians became sick, lost a valuable object, or otherwise needed help, they hired a religious leader called a shaman to perform the Shaking Tent Ceremony. After nightfall, the shaman entered a special round tent and sang and played the drum to call his

Indians developed the kayak, a light, speedy, highly maneuverable craft. The top of the boat was made of hides and fit closely around the paddler's waist, keeping the icy sea water out of the boat.

Some groups, such as the Innu, used the shoulder bones of animals to tell the future. After charring a bone in a fire, they studied the cracks in it. The cracks' shapes and lengths were thought to contain messages about a person's fate.

helpers from the spirit-world. Suddenly, the tent began to shake back and forth wildly, and the voices of the spirit-helpers start speaking out. To onlookers, the spectacle was fun and exciting. They could call out questions for the helpers, who would shout back answers. Sometimes, the spirit-voices would even tell jokes or pose riddles to entertain the crowd.

What is the Arctic?

The Arctic is the stretch of land north of the Subarctic forests. The area is one of the harshest environments in the world. For much of the year, the ground is covered with snow and ice. In January, temperatures can fall as low as 35° below zero. Powerful winds make the frigid air feel even colder and blow up the snow into enormous drifts.

During the dead of winter, there is also very little sunlight. For several months, the sun never rises. The landscape is bathed in twilight for several hours each day, but otherwise the sky is dark.

Who are the Inuit?

The Inuit are the native peoples of the Arctic land stretching from central Alaska to the northern coast of Canada and onto the island of Greenland. Their ancestors came to North America from Asia in about 3,000 B.C., many

The Aleut

The Aleut are the native people of the 1,400-mile Aleutian Island chain off of Alaska's southwest coast. The ancestors of the Aleut came to North America from Asia at about the same time as those of the Inuit. Settling on the isolated Aleutians, however, the Aleut (who call themselves the Unangan) developed their own culture, although it had some similarities to the Inuit way of life. Like the Inuit, the Aleut survived in their windy and wet environment by becoming expert hunters. They were especially re-nowned for their sleek kayaks, from which they harpooned sea otters and other water animals. Their village life, however, had more in common with that of the Indians of the Northwest Coast. The Aleut, like these Indians, grouped people into social ranks that completely determined their wealth and position.

Charms

The Inuit world was full of danger. If a whaler's boat capsized, within minutes he could die in the icy water. If a hunter was careless, even for a moment, a polar bear might maul him to death. If one season's animal catch was small, a family might face starvation.

To protect themselves from the many everyday threats, the Inuit carried small charms. Carved from stone or ivory or crafted from animal hides, each charm had a specific purpose. One charm might make the owner a good seal hunter, while another might drive away evil spirits. Inuit kept their charms with them at all times. Most often, they wore them on a belt or sewed them into their clothes.

thousands of years after the first Indian people arrived on the continent. The Inuit are more closely related to Asians than to other Native American peoples.

The Inuit are better known by the name "Eskimo," a mispronunciation of an Algonquian word meaning "eaters of raw meat." They, however, prefer the term "Inuit," which means "people" in their own language.

How did the Inuit survive in the Arctic?

Over the course of thousands of years, the Inuit learned how to make do with little and to make the most of what they did have. Sources of food and materials for clothing, shelter, and other necessities were meager, so they had to be very attuned to their surroundings to find what was available. To outsiders their homeland might seem a bleak, empty landscape of ice, but to the Inuit, it was a rich, ever-changing environment that offered new opportunities each season.

The Inuit also developed personal characteristics so that they could better cope with hardship. Their society valued patience, good humor, and generosity—qualities that helped them survive when food and other resources were scarce.

What foods did the Inuit traditionally eat?

In their territory, very few plants could grow, so almost all of the Inuit's food came from the fish they caught and the animals they hunted. These animals included whales, seals, walrus, and caribou, a species of deer with huge spiky antlers.

Aside from meat, what did hunting provide the Inuit?

Without many trees or plants in their homeland, the Inuit had to look to animals for most of the materials they needed to make the things they used day to day. To survive in the Arctic, Inuit women crafted heavy coats called parkas from caribou furs and waterproof boots and mittens from sealskins. From whale bones, walrus tusks, and caribou antlers, men made spear tips and other tools. And from blubber, the thick layer of fat below the skin of a whale, the Inuit created fuel oil that they burned for heat and light throughout the harsh winter.

How did the Inuit hunt their prey?

Each animal required a different hunting technique. To hunt caribou, for instance, hunters set up two rows of scarecrowlike figures made of snow. Making as much noise as they could, women and children chased a herd into the area between the scarecrows, which led to a corral or a lake, where hunters waited to spear the frightened animals.

When hunting seals, Inuit hunters looked for clusters of small holes in the ice. These were breathing holes made by seals, who lived below the ice throughout the winter. A seal hunter hunkered by these holes, sometimes for hours, waiting for a seal to approach. When an animal appeared, the hunter stabbed it to death with a harpoon.

The Inuit are better known by the name Eskimo, *a mispronunciation of an Algonquian word meaning "eaters of raw meat." They, however, prefer the term* Inuit, *which means "people" in their own language.*

Whaling usually involved a team of hunters. Led by an expert whale hunter called a *umialik,* about ten men would paddle a boat into the ocean. When they saw a whale, they paddled toward it and shot at it with their harpoons. Pulling on the harpoons, they then dragged the huge animal closer and finished the kill with smaller lances.

Who was Sedna?

In Inuit legend, Sedna was the keeper of the sea creatures the Inuit hunted. As a young woman, against her father's wishes, she married a dog and lived with him on an island. Angry at her betrayal, her father killed her dog-husband and compelled Sedna to sail home with him. On the way, a storm threatened to overturn their boat. Hoping to calm the storm, the father decided to sacrifice his daughter by throwing her into the water. Desperately, Sedna clung to the side of the boat, so her father cut off her fingers with a knife. According to Inuit legend, as they fell into the water, her first joints turned into whales, her second joints became seals, and the rest of the fingers transformed into walruses.

How did the Inuit travel over the ice?

To travel long distances fast, the Inuit used sleds pulled by dogs. For thousands of years, the Inuit bred and trained dogs (later called huskies) that were perfect for this work. Their dogs had four inches of fur that kept them warm even in blizzards. They were also strong. Working in teams of seven or eight, dogs could pull a sled loaded with as much as 800 pounds of cargo.

Dogs also helped in the hunt. Using their well-developed sense of smell, they could track polar bears. When the dogs found a bear, a hunter released their harnesses and let the dogs run toward his prey. With the polar bear distracted by their biting and barking, a hunter could sneak up on the enormous animal and kill it with a knife before it had a chance to attack.

Did all Inuit live in igloos?

Except for those in the far north, the Inuit used igloos—dome-shaped dwellings made from bricks of snow—only as temporary houses while they were on hunting expeditions. Their permanent homes were winter houses built into the side of a hill from sod, wood, bones, or stones. Like igloos, these homes were cleverly constructed to keep the cold air outside. The small entrance was low to the ground and fed into a tunnel, which kept wintry winds from reaching the living space at the tunnel's end. This area was sunk into the ground to provide extra insulation. There was a fire in the center of the living area and the space was furnished with benches that

Inuits used dogs called huskies to pull their sleds when they needed to travel long distances in the severe Arctic environment. The dogs also helped during hunting by cornering and distracting the prey. These men are on a walrus hunt.

were covered with animal skins to make warm and comfortable beds.

In the warmest months of the summer, Inuit stayed in tents. The large tent covers were sewn together from walrus-, caribou-, or sealskins and held up by a pole frame.

How did the Inuit spend the long winter?

To escape the icy cold, the Inuit had to spend much of the winter indoors, but they made the most of this hardship. Comfortable in their warm homes, winter became the season of socializing. Families gathered for feasts and singing and dancing. Both children and adults also loved telling stories and playing games.

Inuit hunters often dressed their dogs in small sealskin boots to protect their paws from sharp ice crystals.

What was a song duel?

A song duel was the Inuit's unique way of settling disputes. Instead of fighting, two people who were angry with

one another came before an audience and took turns singing songs that pointed out the others' faults and weaknesses. Encouraged by the hoots and hollers of the crowd, the singers tried to outdo one another by making the funniest insults.

Learning from the Polar Bear

The Inuit learned how to hunt seals in the summer from an unlikely teacher—the polar bear. Emerging from below the ice after the long winter, seals liked to sunbathe on top of ice floes, where they often fell into a light sleep. When a bear on the hunt slowly crept up to a sleepy seal, he held a paw over his nose. By covering up the only nonwhite part of his body, the bear made himself difficult to see against the white snow and ice. Copying the bear's technique, Inuit hunters likewise camouflaged themselves by wrapping polar bear skins around their bodies.

When the sun hit the Arctic snow, the glare could be blinding. To protect their sight, Inuit wore goggles carved from ivory or wood.

When did non-Indians arrive in the Arctic?

Norsemen from Iceland came to Greenland in 986—almost 500 years before Christopher Columbus sailed to North America. They established two settlements along the southwestern part of the island, which probably was uninhabited at the time. About 100 years later, Inuit people from the north moved close to the Norse settlers. At first the two groups got along, but in time they began to fight one another. The Inuit eventually won the conflict. By 1500, the Norse colonists were gone and their settlements destroyed. Non-Indians did not settle in Greenland again until traders from Denmark established a post there in 1721.

Inuit heated their igloos with simple stone lamps that burned oil made from blubber. These lamps could raise the indoor temperature of a snow house to as high as 90°.

What was the Northwest Passage?

The Northwest Passage was a waterway rumored to run through northern Canada and connect the Atlantic and Pacific Ocean. Beginning in the sixteenth century, Europeans wanted to use the Northwest Passage as a short

route to China, where traders could make a fortune selling European goods. In the late 1500s, the first of a series of expeditions set out in search of the passage. The Europeans did not find it, but they did make another important discovery—that the Inuit were excellent trading partners. The Inuit were eager to trade animal furs for European goods, particularly iron, which made stronger tools than ivory or bone.

British navy officers John Ross and William Edward Parry trade with Inuit in a 1818 drawing by Hans Zakaeus, a Greenland native who served as liaison between the British and the Inuit.

The Printmakers of Cape Dorset

In the late 1950s, the Inuits of the small community of Cape Dorset were poor and often hungry. Their fortunes changed when James Houston, a non-Indian writer, introduced them to the art of printmaking. Although this art form was new to the Cape Dorset Inuit, they took to it immediately. In their prints, they made use of the same simple patterns that traditionally they had used to decorate their sealskin clothing.

The most famous of the Cape Dorset printmakers is Kenojuak, the first woman to master the art. Best known for her prints of animals, two of her works—*The Enchanted Owl* and *Return of the Sun*—have appeared on Canadian postage stamps. In recognition of her contributions to art, in 1967 she was given the Order of Canada, the highest honor awarded to civilians by that country.

Flowering Beads

In the mid-1800s, Catholic nuns came to Chipewyan territory to teach the Indians about their religion. At the same time, the nuns instructed the Indians in a new craft—floral embroidery. Chipewyan women already decorated their clothes with dyed porcupine quills, but they were difficult to work with. They found the thread and beads given to them by non-Indians much easier to sew into curving forms. Soon their favorite pattern became brilliant and beautiful floral shapes modeled on the wild flowers of their homeland.

How did trading change native life?

Aside from new trade goods, non-Indian traders brought with them European diseases. Like other native populations, the Inuit suffered many deaths because of these foreign germs. Others were killed in violent encounters with nonnatives. The Aleut were particularly threatened by the Russian traders who came to their lands in the 1740s.

Over time, trading with non-Indians also began to change where the Inuit lived and how they spent their time. Many left their old communities to move nearer to trading posts and began hunting more and more to have something to trade. They also started hunting whatever animal would bring the best price. For instance, in the nineteenth century, whale hunting increased because whites wanted baleen—the jawbone of the bowhead whale, which they used to make umbrella ribs, mattresses, and buggy whips. As a result, the Inuit overhunted whales, and many natives plunged into poverty whenever the price of baleen fell.

When did Subarctic Indians encounter whites?

Whites first arrived in the eastern Subarctic in the sixteenth and seventeenth centuries. Encounters came later in western regions. Many Subarctic groups did not meet whites until the nineteenth century.

The first whites in their lands were traders. They were soon followed by missionaries who wanted to convert the Indians to Christianity. Other whites began to settle in the

Indians' traditional homelands, threatening their homes and their culture. In the twentieth century, after their territory became part of Canada, many Indian groups have fought for the Canadian government to recognize their claim to their land.

Who were the Métis?

In the 1700s, many Indian women married white fur traders. From their children emerged a new Subarctic group known as the Métis, after the French word for "mixed." Mostly of mixed Cree and French ancestry, the Métis developed a unique culture that blended Indian and white ways.Beginning in the early nineteenth century, the Métis had settled the Red River area of present-day Manitoba, Canada.

When the Dominion of Canada was formed in 1867, the Métis were afraid the new Canadian government would let whites take over their lands. To stop it, the Métis rebelled against Canada and set up their own government led by Louis Riel Jr. Canada, however, decided to fight the rebels. In 1885 at the Battle of Batoche, the rebels and the Métis's dream of independence was crushed. Riel was hanged for treason, but he is still considered a hero by the Métis, whose fight for their land continues today.

Are the natives of the Arctic and Subarctic still hunters?

Although they now generally make most of their income from wage work, many native people still hunt for their livelihood. But, with their introduction to new goods,

Land for Alaska's Natives

When Alaska became a state in 1959, the U.S. government took control of more than one-fourth of the new state's land. Much of the area was claimed by native Alaskans, but they were given no money for it. In 1971, Congress tried to right this wrong by passing the Alaska Native Claims Settlement Act. This law returned 44,000,000 acres of land to native groups. They were also given $462.5 million and rights to future mineral and oil income worth about $500 million.

The World Eskimo-Indian Olympics

Every year at the end of July, Fairbanks, Alaska, hosts the World Eskimo-Indian Olympics, an event that draws Inuit and Indian athletes from throughout the state. The participants compete in traditional games and contests, including:

The Ear Pull: A three-foot-long loop of string is placed around the right ear of two competitors sitting on the floor. Each pulls back in a tug-of-war to try to force the string to slip off of his or her opponent's ear.

Drop the Bomb: Competitors lie facedown on the floor, stretching out their arms and legs. Teams of three men then lift each about a foot off the ground and carry him or her along a measured path. The winner is the competitor whose body remains stiff for the longest distance.

The Knuckle Hop: As if doing a push-up, competitors rest their knuckles and toes on the floor. In this position, they hop forward, trying to travel farther than their opponents.

the way they hunt has changed. Rifles or guns that shoot out a harpoon with an explosive charge have replaced the spears and harpoons formerly made by hand. Fiberglass boats with outboard motors have replaced the old whaling vessels and kayaks. And snowmobiles are far more common than sleds led by teams of dogs. But all these innovations have not destroyed their hunting traditions. The same hardiness and resilience that allowed these peoples to live in an icy wilderness also help them retain their old ways in a changing world.

A determined contestant competes in the knuckle hop event at the World Eskimo-Indian Olympics in Fairbanks, Alaska. The annual four-day games test skill, strength, and endurance in a variety of Inuit sports passed down from one generation to the next.

How many Native Americans now live in the United States? ◆ What are the largest Native American tribes? ◆ Where do Native Americans live? ◆ What do they do for a living? What is the average income of a Native American family? ◆ Why do so many reservation Native Americans have a low income? ◆ What are Native Americans doing to improve conditions on reservations? ◆ Why do so many tribes run casinos? ◆ What is pan-Indianism? ◆ What was Red Power? ◆ What is self-determination? ◆ What is repatriation? ◆ What are Indian land claims? ◆ Are Native Americans U.S. citizens? ◆ What is federal recognition? ◆ Do

NATIVE AMERICANS TODAY

How many Native Americans now live in the United States?

According to the 1990 census, there are about 1,900,000 Native Americans in the United States—approximately .75 percent of the total U.S. population. The Native American population has grown steadily throughout the twentieth century. It now stands at more than four times its lowest point in about 1900. Native Americans then numbered only 400,000, just .5 percent of all the people in the country.

Who are the Natives of Canada?

Canada's 1996 census found that about 2.75 percent of its citizens belong to three different native groups. It counted approximately 535,000 Indians, 41,000 Inuit, and 210,000 Métis. The descendants of Indians and European (mostly French) traders, the Métis developed their own unique culture in western Canada during the nineteenth century.

What are the largest Native American tribes?

The 1990 census listed four tribes with populations of more than 100,000: the Cherokee at 308,000, the Navajo at 219,000, the Ojibwa (also known as the Chippewa) at 104,000, and the Sioux at 103,000.

In addition to about 31,000 American Indians, Alaska is the home of people from two other native groups— the Inuit (44,000) and Aleut (10,000).

Where do Native Americans live?

As of 1990 nearly half of all Native Americans in the United States lived west of the Mississippi River. The states with the biggest Native American populations were Oklahoma (13.2 percent), California (12.7 percent), Arizona (10.7 percent), and New Mexico (7.0 percent).

Only about one in every five Native Americans lived on one of the 314 reservations in the United States. The reservation with the biggest population is the Navajo Indian Reservation (143,000) in Arizona and New Mexico. The next three largest are the Pine Ridge Indian Reservation (11,000) in South Dakota, the Fort Apache Indian Reservation (10,000) in Arizona, and the Gila River Indian Reservation (9,000), also in Arizona.

What do they do for a living?

By and large, Native Americans work at the same types of jobs as all other Americans. A high percentage, though, are factory workers, repair people, and other skilled technicians. Many Native Americans have gone into these fields because, beginning in the 1950s, the government offered them free or low-cost vocational training. A large number of Native Americans also work for the Bureau of Indian Affairs (BIA), the government agency that oversees U.S. dealings with Indian peoples, because the BIA has a policy of giving preference to Indian job applicants. Many other Native Americans are employed as artists and craftspeople. Following the artistic traditions of their people, these artists make paintings, baskets, pottery, jewelry, blankets, and other decorative items for sale.

The Native American population in the United States is expected to double by the year 2050.

Native Americans in the City

The U.S. cities with the highest Native American populations are:

Los Angeles, California	87,000	New York, New York	46,000
Tulsa, Oklahoma	48,000	Oklahoma City, Oklahoma	46,000
		San Francisco, California	41,000

What is the average income of a Native American family?

The U.S. census of 1990 found that the average Native American family makes about $21,750, far below the average income of all American families ($35,225). About 27 percent of Native American families live in poverty. Native Americans on reservations are the most impoverished. Just over half of all reservation residents live below the poverty level set by the U.S. government.

Why do so many reservation Native Americans have a low income?

The poverty on most reservations is rooted in the past. In earlier centuries, as land was taken away from Native Americans, so were their traditional ways of feeding their families. Many people had difficulty finding a new way to make a living on a reservation. Much of the land on reservations was of very poor quality, so occupations such as farming and ranching were often out of reach. Some Indians tried working for wages, but white-run businesses often refused to hire Indians, and with very little money or education, few Native Americans could start businesses of their own.

During the late twentieth century, many Native Americans have left reservations to find work in cities. But

Famous Native American Artists

Ben Nighthorse Campbell (Northern Cheyenne, born 1933): Campbell's jewelry combines Native American and Japanese traditions. In addition to being a well-known jewelry designer, he is a distinguished U.S. Senator from Montana.

Harry Fonseca (Maidu, born 1946): Fonseca is best known for his humorous paintings of Coyote, a character in many Native American myths whose misadventures traditionally taught Indians lessons about good and bad behavior.

Shelley Niro (Mohawk, born 1954): Niro, a photographer and film-maker, uses playful self-portraits to explore the world of modern Native American women.

Jaune Quick-to-See Smith (Flathead-Cree-Shoshone, born 1940): The famed painter Smith uses her art to protest the mistreatment of Indian peoples in the past and present.

others are so attached to their land and their communities that they would rather live in poverty than leave their homes.

What are Native Americans doing to improve conditions on reservations?

Across North America, tribal governments and activist groups are trying to help make the lives of reservation Native Americans better. They have created many programs dedicated to improving the housing, education, and employment opportunities available on reservations.

Many of these programs are funded by the federal government, but others are financed by business concerns run by tribes. In recent years, the most profitable tribal businesses have been casinos and bingo parlors.

Why do so many tribes run casinos?

Reservation residents have to follow laws made by the U.S. government, but not those made by states. Many states outlaw casinos or at least place complicated rules on how they can be run. But because tribes do not have to follow state laws, they can establish casinos on reservations with little interference. Aside from some regulations set by the U.S. government, tribes are largely free to operate these businesses as they choose.

Since the 1980s, many Native Americans tribes have opened casinos and gambling parlors. Some have been very successful, giving a big financial boost to tribes and providing jobs for tribe members. Although some Native

The Foxwoods Casino

In 1992, the small Mashantucket Pequot tribe opened the Foxwoods Casino and Resort in Connecticut. The business was such a success that, within a few years, it was bringing in almost $1 billion a year. In addition to helping other tribes establish their own businesses, the tribe has used its profits to build a $193 million museum and research center on its reservation. Dedicated in August 1998, the huge museum complex features interactive films and videos and a re-creation of a traditional Pequot village.

The Case of Leonard Peltier

An activist belonging to the American Indian Movement, Leonard Peltier was convicted in 1976 of murdering two FBI agents on South Dakota's Pine Ridge Indian Reservation. He was sentenced to two consecutive life terms in prison.

Many people around the world believe that Peltier is innocent. Seeing him as a political prisoner of the U.S. government, Peltier's supporters have spent more than 20 years campaigning for his case to be reexamined.

Americans oppose the casinos because they think gambling is wrong, others are pleased by how casino income has helped their tribes to prosper.

What is pan-Indianism?

Pan-Indianism is a term that refers to Native American peoples from many different tribes working together as though they were one people. This idea is fairly new. Before non-Indians came to North America, there were at least 300 tribes and many more smaller groups. Some were allies, but many were enemies. As a result, when non-Indians began attacking Indians or trying to take away their land, tribes sometimes sided with whites against their Indian enemies.

Pan-Indian rights groups, such as the Society of American Indians, first formed in the early twentieth century, when many Indian tribes were living in poverty. At that time, Indians came to realize that their tribal differences were small in comparison to the larger problems of discrimination and destitution that they shared. Since that time, Native Americans from different tribes have formed many Pan-Indian groups that have had great success in fighting for the rights of all natives.

What was Red Power?

In the late 1960s and early 1970s, many young Indians joined together to protest the way Indians were treated by non-Indians and the U.S. government. Their efforts became known as the Red Power movement. The name was drawn

In spring 1978, the American Indian Movement organized "The Longest Walk," a march from San Francisco to Washington, D.C., to promote Native American rights. In late July, after five months on the road, several hundred marchers representing approximately 80 different tribes reached the nation's capital.

from the Black Power movement, a similar fight that was then being waged by African American activists.

With many dramatic protests, the Red Power movement brought worldwide attention to the problems of contemporary Native Americans. Largely because of these activists' efforts, the United States adopted a new policy of self-determination toward Native Americans.

What is self-determination?

In the past, the U.S. government had always dictated to Indians how they should behave, what they should learn in school, what jobs they should work, and how their lands should be used. The policy of self-determination of the 1970s reversed this thinking. Self-determination meant that Indians should determine for themselves how government funds could be used to improve their lives. As a result, since the mid-1970s, Native Americans have been able to take control of programs designed to give them better education, jobs, housing, and health care.

What is repatriation?

Repatriation refers to one of the issues most important to Native Americans today—the return to tribes of ancient

Indian bones and artifacts. In the past, non-Indians freely dug up Indian burial sites, and many of the remains they uncovered ended up in museums. To Native Americans, museum displays of their ancestors' skeletons were deeply offensive. For many decades, they fought to have these bones returned to their descendants, so they could be reburied properly.

In 1990, the U.S. Congress passed a sweeping law that has compelled many museums to repatriate Indian remains. The law—known as the Native American Graves Protection and Repatriation Act—has also forced the return of masks, rattles, and other objects of religious importance that were stolen from Indian graves. Having possession of these sacred objects once again has inspired several tribes to revive old ceremonies and tribal customs.

What are Indian land claims?

Throughout American history, the United States has taken over lands claimed by Indians without consulting the peoples who lived there. As a result, in the twentieth century many Indians took the United States to court, insisting that the country give them their land back or at least pay them fairly for it.

Some Indian land claims have been resolved, but many more remain pending. One still in the courts is the Lakota Sioux's campaign for the return of the Black Hills, an area that to them is sacred. In 1980 the U.S. Supreme Court offered the Lakota more than $100 million to compensate them for the Black Hills region. But

Kennewick Man

In July 1996, a college student stumbled upon something remarkable on the banks of the Columbia River in Washington State: a human skeleton that was more than 9,000 years old. Named Kennewick Man after a nearby town, five tribes in the region claim the skeleton as an ancestor.

While non-Indian scientists made plans to study the bones, these tribes fought in the courts for the right to Kennewick Man, whom they call the Ancient One. To show proper respect for this ancestor, they want to rebury the skeleton using traditional Indian funeral rituals.

Nunavut

On April 1, 1999, Nunavut became a new territory of Canada. This area, which had been the eastern half of the Northwest Territories, is the home of most of Canada's Inuit, the native group sometimes called Eskimos. With the creation of Nunavut (meaning "our land" in Inuktitut, the Inuit language), the Inuit have been given far more say in how they are governed.

Some Iroquois travel the globe without a U.S. passport. They instead use passports issued by the Iroquois nation, which many foreign countries recognize as an independent country.

the Lakota refused to take the money. They want nothing less than the land itself and continue their legal battle for it.

Are Native Americans U.S. citizens?

Since 1924, any Native American born in the United States has been legally considered a citizen. Native Americans that belong to tribes recognized by the federal government are also citizens of these tribal nations. Many Native Americans, though, consider themselves tribal citizens first, and U.S. citizens second.

What is federal recognition?

An Indian group has federal recognition when the U.S. government defines it as a tribe. Having federal recognition is important because only federally recognized tribes can receive certain funds and benefits reserved for Native Americans.

Some Native American groups that consider themselves tribes do not have federal recognition because they do not meet the government's standards. For instance, if a group has its own area of land or in the past negotiated a treaty with the United States, the government is likely to give it tribal status. But many groups have no land base or treaty because the U.S. government took their land without their consent. In recent years, unrecognized tribes such as the Lumbee of North Carolina have taken their case to court to force the United States to give them the recognition they have long been denied.

Do Native Americans still speak Indian languages?

Some Native Americans are bilingual. They speak English with non-Indians but might use their native language with relatives and other tribe members. In some Native American communities, however, an Indian language is rarely heard. Many Native Americans stopped using their own languages because of pressure from U.S. officials. Until recently, for instance, Indian students attending government schools would be severely punished if they said a word in the language of their tribe.

As a result, some Indian languages are in danger of being forgotten forever. To preserve them, tribes have started programs to teach their languages to their children, who can then pass along this knowledge to future generations.

What is a powwow?

A powwow is a festival where Indians from different tribes come together to celebrate their heritage. The main attraction at powwows are exhibitions of Indian singing and dancing. Especially exciting are fancy dancing competitions, during which elaborately costumed dancers display spectacular movements inspired by traditional dances.

Some powwows are small gatherings that last an afternoon. Others are huge annual events held over several days that attract an audience of thousands, including both Indians and non-Indians. Big powwows include the Red Earth Festival in Oklahoma City, Oklahoma, the Gathering of Nations in Albuquerque, New Mexico, and the American Indian Exposition in Anadarko, Oklahoma.

What is the Native American Church?

The Native American Church is a religion that combines some Christian beliefs with the Indian peyote religion that grew up in the nineteenth century. Peyote is a part of a cactus that grows wild in the Southwest. By eating peyote, members of the Native American Church have visions that they believe bring them closer to God.

For more than 100 years, whites have tried to outlaw peyote use, maintaining that peyote is a dangerous drug.

Famous Native American Writers

Louise Erdrich (Chippewa, born 1954): In best-sellers such as *Love Medicine* and *Tracks*, Erdrich writes stories about three generations of Indians living in North Dakota.

Joy Harjo (Creek, born 1951): Harjo is an acclaimed poet whose books include *She Had Some Horses* and *In Mad Love and War*. With her band Poetic Justice, she also performs songs based on her poems.

N. Scott Momaday (Kiowa, born 1934): A well-known Native American novelist, Momaday won the Pulitzer Prize in 1969 for his book *House Made of Dawn*.

Leslie Marmon Silko (Laguna Pueblo, born 1948): The author of *Ceremony* and other novels, Silko often retells traditional Pueblo stories in her works.

To the Indians who belong to the Native American Church, however, it is a sacrament that allows them to have an experience absolutely necessary to the practice of their religion. Throughout the twentieth century,

With the publication of his novel *House Made of Dawn* (1968) and autobiography *The Way to Rainy Mountain* (1968), Kiowa writer N. Scott Momaday ushered in a new era in Native American literature. Following his example, many talented young Native American writers turned to fiction and poetry to depict Native American life and celebrate tribal traditions.

Director Chris Eyre (left) and writer Sherman Alexie discuss a scene in *Smoke Signals* (1998), the first feature film written, produced, and directed by Native Americans.

Native American Church members have had to fight in court for the right to use peyote in their religious ceremonies.

What is the National Museum of the American Indian?

In 1989, the U.S. Congress passed a law calling for the creation of a new museum as a "living memorial to Native Americans and their traditions." Part of the Smithsonian Institution, the new National Museum of the American Indian is being built next to the U.S. Capitol Building on

Famous Native American Performers

Tantoo Cardinal (Métis, born 1950): One of Canada's most celebrated actresses, Cardinal has appeared in the films *Black Robe* and *Legends of the Fall* and the television movies *Lakota Woman* and *Tecumseh*.

Graham Greene (Oneida, born 1952): A veteran of film and theater, Greene was nominated for an Academy Award for his performance as Kicking Bird in *Dances with Wolves*.

R. Carlos Nakai (Navajo-Ute, born 1946): In his original songs, the flutist Nakai meshes melodies played on the Native American flute with synthesized music, nature sounds, and Indian singing.

Joanne Shenandoah (Oneida, born 1960): Through her music, Shenandoah reinterprets Iroquois songs with her striking voice and unique blend of traditional and contemporary instrumentation.

the last remaining plot on the National Mall in Washington, D.C. The museum, scheduled to open in 2002, will house a collection of more 1,000,000 Native American artifacts and works of art.

How is the depiction of Indians in movies changing?

Soon after the film was invented, an entire industry grew up around westerns—films about Indian-white conflicts on the Plains. These movies almost always depicted Plains Indians as villainous, bloodthirsty savages. Audiences were encouraged to cheer when whites killed them and took over their lands.

Beginning in the late 1960s, non-Indian filmmakers began to create stories of the Plains Wars that were far more sympathetic to the Indians involved. *Little Big Man* (1970) and *Dances with Wolves* (1990), for instance, were celebrated for depicting Indians as full characters and for casting Indian actors in these parts. But even these films showed Indian culture from the perspective of non-Indian characters. Only in recent years have Native American filmmakers such as Sherman Alexie and Alanis Obomoswin begun to create movies that tell Indian stories from an Indian point of view.

This model shows the design for the National Museum of the American Indian, slated to open ont he Mall in Washington, D.C. in 2002. The lead architect is Douglas Cardinal, a Canadian Indian of Blackfoot and Métis ancestry.

Buffy Sainte-Marie

In the 60s, Cree singer-songwriter Buffy Sainte-Marie was one of America's favorite folk artists. With her passionate lyrics and dynamic singing style, she electrified audiences with her songs of protest. In many of her most popular songs—such as "Native American Child," "Now That the Buffalo's Gone," and "My Country 'Tis of Thy People You're Dying"—she spoke out against the many injustices suffered by Native Americans throughout North American history.

Beginning in 1975, Sainte-Marie took on a second career as an actress. From 1976 to 1981, Sainte-Marie was a cast member of the children's television series *Sesame Street*. She has also appeared in the television films *Son of Morning Star* and *The Broken Chain*.

During the 1990s, Sainte-Marie has explored the creative possibilities of the computer. She records music from her own home studio in Hawaii and creates paintings by scanning nineteenth-century photographs of Indians and using her computer to color the pictures. In 1996, she established the Cradleboard Teaching Project, an educational program that allows Indian and non-Indians students to talk with one another over the Internet.

What is the most common misconception about Native Americans today?

Many non-Indians believe that Native Americans are a "vanishing race," a group of people rooted so firmly in the past that they are doomed to die out. In fact, the opposite is true. The Native American population throughout the continent is on the rise. Native Americans, too, are working harder than ever to make sure their voices are heard. As more and more Native Americans are educated as lawyers, doctors, teachers, and journalists, they are finding new ways to fight discrimination and command respect for Indian beliefs and traditions.

GLOSSARY

A
adobe bricks made of clay used by some Southwest Indians to construct buildings
agent a U.S. official hired to oversee an Indian reservation
agency the building on a reservation where an agent lives and works
Aleut the native people of the Aleutian island chain of Alaska
American Indian Movement a group of Indian activists who in the late 1960s and 1970s protested the U.S. government's mistreatment of Indians
anthropologist a scholar who studies human societies
archaeologist a scholar who studies ancient people

C
clan a group of tribe members who believe they have a common ancestor
copper a flat, shield-like object made out of copper metal by some Northwestern Indian tribes, such as the Kwakiutl; they believed coppers held the souls of their ancestors.
creation story ancient story that tells of how an Indian tribe came into existence
culture the customs and beliefs that define a group of people's way of life

D
dugout a canoe made by setting a log on fire, then scooping out the soft, charred wood

F
federal recognition the United State's official acknowledgment of a group of Indians as a tribe that is eligible for government funds and benefits
Five Civilized Tribes the Cherokee, Chickasaw, Choctaw, Creek, and Seminole
fur trade trading arrangement dating from the late 1500s, in which Indians gave Europeans furs in exchange for manufactured goods, such as metal tools, cloth, and guns

H
hogan a round one-room house made from wood poles and mud by the Navajo
homeland an Indian tribe's original territory

I
igloo a dome-shaped dwelling made from blocks of ice by the Inuit
Indian the native peoples of North America whose ancestors came from Asia about 12,000 to 60,000 years ago; also called Native Americans
Indian Territory an area west of the Mississippi River where Indians from other regions (mostly the Southeast) were relocated; by 1854, its boundaries were roughly the same as those of present-day Oklahoma

Inuit the native peoples of the Arctic whose ancestors came to North America from Asia about 5,000 years ago

Iroquois Confederacy the alliance of the Cayuga, Mohawk, Oneida, Onondaga, and Seneca formed in about 1400; the Tuscaroras joined in 1722

K

kiva an underground chamber where the Pueblo Indians hold ceremonies

L

longhouse a large barn-shaped dwelling made from saplings covered with bark shingles by the Iroquois

M

Métis a person of Indian and European (usually French) ancestry

missionary a person seeking to convert another person to their religion (for example, someone who tries to persuade an Indian to practice Christianity)

mission a religious center where missionaries try to convert others to their religion (for example, the buildings constructed by Catholic priests for California Indians between 1769 and 1834)

N

Native American a term meaning "Indian" in popular use since the late 1960s

Native Canadian term for an Indian, an Inuit, or a Métis

P

potlatch Northwest Indian ceremonies during which wealthy hosts gave food and gifts to their guests

pow-wow a festival where Indians from different tribes come together to celebrate their heritage.

pueblo a clay-walled, multi-family dwelling made by the Pueblo Indians

R

Red Power movement led by young Indian activists in the late 1960s and 1970s that protested the mistreatment of Indians by non-Indians

relocation U.S. policy of the 1950s and 1960s that encouraged reservation Indians to move to cities

removal U.S. policy of the 1830s that forced Southeastern Indian tribes to relocate to lands west of the Mississippi River

repatriation the return of Indian bones and ceremonial items held in museums to the tribes they came from

reservation an area of land set aside by the U.S. government for the exclusive use of a group of Indians

S

self-determination U.S. policy, established in the mid-1970s, that allows Indians to determine for themselves how government funds due to them should be spent

T

termination U.S. policy of the 1950s that sought to dissolve Indian reservations

tipi a cone-shaped house made from a hide cover placed over a pole frame used by Plains Indians

totem pole a giant sculpture made by Northwest Indians by carving images of humans, animals, and beings from the spirit world onto the truck of a tree

Trail of Tears the 1838 relocation of the Cherokee from their homeland in the Southeast to what is now Oklahoma (then called Indian Territory)

treaty a written agreement between two or more nations (an Indian tribe and the U.S. government, for instance)

tribe a group of related Indians who share the same language, religious beliefs, and social customs

W

wampum small purple and white shell beads that were used as money by Northeast Indians

wigwam a cone-shaped house made of saplings covered with grass mats or bark shingles that were built by the Algonquian tribes of the Northeast

Wounded Knee site of the 1890 massacre of about three hundred Sioux and Cheyenne by U.S. troops; also, site of a 1973 protest organized by the American Indian Movement

SELECTED BIBLIOGRAPHY

American Indians, 3 vols. Pasadena, Ca.: Salem Press, 1995.

Bataille, Gretchen M., ed. *Native American Women*. New York: Garland, 1993.

Bonvillain, Nancy. *The Inuit*. New York: Chelsea House, 1995.

Champagne, Duane. *Native America: Portrait of the Peoples*. Detroit: Visible Ink Press, 1994.

—————, ed. *Chronology of Native North American History*. Detroit: Gale Research, 1994.

Davis, Mary B., ed. *Native America in the Twentieth Century: An Encyclopedia*. New York: Garland Publishing, 1996.

Editors of Time-Life Books. *The American Indians*, 10 vols. Alexandria, Va.: Time-Life Books, 1992-94.

Encyclopedia of North American Indians, 11 vols. New York: Marshall Cavendish, 1997.

Feest, Christian F. *Native Arts of North America*. New York: Oxford University Press, 1980.

Gill, Sam D., and Irene F. Sullivan. *Dictionary of Native American Mythology*. Santa Barbara, Ca.: ABC-CLIO, 1992.

Graymont, Barbara. *The Iroquois*. New York: Chelsea House, 1988.

Hazen-Hammond, Susan. *Timelines of Native American History*. New York: Perigee, 1997.

Hoxie, Frederick E., ed. *Encyclopedia of North American Indians*. Boston: Houghton Mifflin, 1996.

Iverson, Peter. *The Navajo*. New York: Chelsea House: 1990.

Kelly, Lawrence C. *Federal Indian Policy*. New York: Chelsea House, 1990.

Malinowski, Sharon, ed. *Notable Native Americans*. Detroit: Gale Research, 1995.

Mattheissen, Peter. *In the Spirit of Crazy Horse*. New York: Viking Penguin, 1991.

Miller, Mary Ellen. *The Art of Mesoamerica*. London: Thames and Hudson, 1986.

Nabokov, Peter, ed. *Native American Testimony*. New York: Viking, 1991.

————, and Robert Easton. *Native American Architecture*. New York: Oxford University Press, 1989.

Nies, Judith. *Native American History*. New York: Ballantine Books, 1996.

Ortiz, Alfonso. *The Pueblo*. New York: Chelsea House, 1994.

Paisano, Edna L. *We the First Americans*. Washington, D.C., Bureau of the Census, 1993.

Perdue, Theda. *The Cherokee*. New York: Chelsea House, 1989.

Snow, Dean. *The Archaeology of North America*. New York: Chelsea House, 1988.

Sonneborn, Liz. *A to Z of Native American Women*. New York: Facts on File, 1998.

Sturtevant, William C., ed. *Handbook of North American Indians*, 11 vols. Smithsonian Institution: Washington, D.C., 1978-98.

Utley, Robert M. *The Indian Frontier of the American West, 1846-1890*. Albuquerque: University of New Mexico Press, 1984.

————, and Wilcomb E. Washburn. *Indian Wars*. Boston: Houghton Mifflin, 1977.

Waldman, Carl. *Atlas of the North American Indian*. New York: Facts on File, 1985.

————. *Encyclopedia of Native American Tribes*. New York: Facts on File, 1988.

————. *Who Was Who in Native American History*. New York: Facts on File, 1990.

THE NEW YORK PUBLIC LIBRARY'S RECOMMENDED READING LIST

Cwiklik, Robert. *Sequoyah and the Cherokee Alphabet*. Englewood Cliffs, NJ. Silver Burdett Press, 1989

Freedman, Russell. *The Life and Death of Crazy Horse*. New York. Holiday House, 1996

Gale Encyclopedia of Native American Tribes. Detroit. Gale, 1998

Grant, Bruce. *American Indians, Yesterday and Today*. New York. Dutton, 1960

Griffin-Pierce, Trudy. *The Encyclopedia of Native America*. New York. Viking, 1995

Holler, Anne. *Pocahontas, Powhatan Peacemaker*. New York. Chelsea House, 1993

Immell, Myra. *Tecumseh*. San Diego, CA. Lucent Books, 1997

In a Sacred Manner I Live: Native American Wisdom. New York. Viking, 1995

McClard, Megan. *Hiawatha and the Iroquois League*. Englewood Cliffs, NJ. Silver Burdett Press, 1989

Marrin, Albert. *Plains Warrior: Chief Quanah Parker and the Comanches*. New York. Atheneum Books for Young Readers, 1996

Moquin, Wayne. *Great Documents in American Indian History*. New York. Praeger, 1973

Sattler, Helen Roney. *The Earliest Americans*. New York. Clarion Books, 1993

Schleichert, Elizabeth. *Sitting Bull: Sioux Leader*. Springfield, NJ. Enslow Publishers, 1997

Schwartz, Melissa. *Geronimo: Apache Warrior*. New York. Chelsea House, 1992

Sherman, Josepha. *First Americans: Spirit of the Land and the People.* New York. Smithmark, 1996

We Rode the Wind: Recollections of Native American Life. Minneapolis. Runestone Press, 1995

Weatherford, Jack. *Native Roots: How the Indian Nourished America.* New York. Crown, 1991

White, Alana. *Sacagawea: Westward with Lewis and Clark.* Springfield, NJ. Enslow, 1997

Wood, Marion. *Ancient America.* New York. Facts on File, 1990

The World of the American Indian. Washington, D.C. National Geographic Society, 1993

Yates, Diana. *Chief Joseph: Thunder Rolling Down from the Mountains.* Staten Island, NY. Ward Hill Press, 1992

INDEX

Note: Page numbers in *italics* indicate illustrations.

A

Abenaki, 29
acorns, 100, 101
activism, 81, 82, 107-8, 143-44,
    144, 151
Adena Culture, 12, 13, 14
adobe, 12, 87 (*see also* clay-
    walled houses; pueblos)
adoption, 34, 40, 43, 69,
    76
    by non-Indian parents, 79,
    80
African American slaves, 57,
    59
afterlife beliefs, 10, 14
agriculture. *See* farming
Ahyokeh, 57
AIM. *See* American Indian
    Movement
Akimel O'Oodham (Pima), 10,
    83, 93
Alabama, 51, 59, 62
Alaska, 109, 125, 128, 137, 138,
    139
Alaska Native Claims
    Settlement Act, 137
Alberta (Canada), 65
Alcatraz takeover, 107-8
alcoholism, 77
Aleut, 128, 136
Aleutian Islands, 128
Alexie, Sherman, *149*, 150
Algonquian, 29-32, 34, 36, 129,
    130
alligators, *52*
alphabet
    Cherokee, *58*
    Navajo Code Talker, 94
American Indian Movement,
    82, 143, *144*
American Revolution, 44-45

American settlers, 44-45, 71,
    105, 121
Anasazi, 10-11, 83
animals
    carved designs, *9*, 14, 113-
    14, *114*, 115
    as clan names, 35
    hide-covered shield designs,
    70
    Inuit prints, 135
    Mogollon beliefs, 10
    Subarctic beliefs, 126-27,
    128
    See also hunters; *specific
    types*
anthropologists, 5, 106-7
Apache, 65, 83, 84
Arapaho, 65, 77, *77*, 78
archaeologists, 5, 7, 10
Arctic Circle, 125
Arctic Indians, 128-35, 137-38
Arizona, 8, 9, 10, 12, 83, 89,
    93, 95, 140
arrows, 69
art
    Aztec, 26, 28
    birch-bark, 33
    Cape Dorset prints, 135
    cave, 5, 98, *98*
    current artists, 140, 151
    decorated shells, *9*, 14
    Fort Marion drawings, 78
    Navajo drypaintings, 91
    Northwest Indians, 112-13
    Toltec, 23
    See also crafts; sculpture
artifacts, 10, 13, 14, 145-46,
    150
Asia, 5-6, 128, 129
assimilation, 64, 81
astronomy, 21-22

Atlantic Coast, 29, 37
Aztec, 17, 18, 20, 24-28

B

baby baskets, 101
baleen, 136
ball courts, 10, 22, 55
basalt, *19*, 20
Basket Making period, 10
baskets
    Anasazi, 10
    California Indians, 101-2,
    102
    Southeast Indians, 52
Battle of Batoche, 137
Battle of Little Bighorn, 73-74,
    75
Battle of the Thames, 46
Battle of Tippecanoe, 47
beads, 43-44, 136
beans, 8, 14, 36, 51
beaver, 42, 125
Beaver Wars, 42-43
Belize, 17, 20
Bella Bella, 109, 117
Beloved Woman, 56
Beothuk, 37
Bering land bridge, 7
Bering Strait, 6
berries, 31, 99, 122
Big Foot, 79
Biloxi, 51
birch bark, 31, 33
Black Drink, 52, 56
Black Elk, 81
Black Elk Speaks (Neihardt),
    81
Blackfeet, 65, 68, *69*, 73
Black Hills (S.D.), 72-73, 82,
    145-46
black-on-black pottery, 91

Black Robes (Jesuits), 44
Black World, 6
blankets, 9, 92, 94, 114
Blessingway, 90, 91
blood sacrifice, 18, 22, 23, 26
blubber, 130, 134
Blue-Green World, 6
Boldt decision (1974), 122-23
bones and artifacts, 145
Booger Dance, 56
Bosque Redondo, 93
bows and arrows, 70
Bozeman Trail, 71
Brant, Joseph (chief), 45
breath master (fire), 53
British. *See* English colonists;
   English traders
British Columbia, 109
Brown Weasel Woman, 73
buffalo, 65, 66, *66*, 67, 71, 72,
   78
   hunting methods, 67, 68
   near extinction, 76-77
   return of, 82
   uses, 68, 71
Buffalo Bill's Wild West Show,
   75-76
bulbs, hyacinth, 100
bulrush (tule), 100
Bureau of Indian Affairs, 47,
   140
burial in canoes, 117
burial mounds, 13, 14
burial sites, 145

C

Cabot, John, 37
Cabrillo, Juan, 102
Cahokia, 15-16
Cahuilla, 99
Caitlin, George, 66
calendars, 21-22, 69
California
   American settlers, 105
   current Native population,
      140
   Gold Rush, 93, 105-6
California Indians, 97-108
   contact with non-Indians,
      102-5, 106
   current population, 107-8
   landless tribes, 106
   Spanish missions, 103-5,
      103
camouflage, 133

Campbell, Ben Nighthorse,
   141
Canada, 29, 32, 37, 43, 48, 65,
   69, 74, 81
   current Native population,
      139
   Inuit, 128, 135, 146
   Métis, 137, 139
   "Natives" terminology, 3
   Northwest Indians, 109
   Northwest Passage quest,
      134-36
   Nunavut territory, 146
   Subarctic Indians, 125, 137
candlefish (eulachon), 112
Cannibal-at-the-North-End-of-
   the-World, *116*, 118
canoe-burial, 117
canoes, 31
Cape Dorset, 135
captivity narrative, 41
Cardinal, Douglas, *150*
Cardinal, Tantoo, 149
caribou, 125, 130, 132
Carleton, James A., 93
carving. *See* sculpture; wood
   carving
Casa Grande, 9-10
casinos, 142-43
Catawba, 51, 53, 61
Catholicism
   Aztec descendants, 28
   California missions, 103-5,
      103
   Mohawk convert, 44
   Pueblo conversion efforts,
      88, 89
   Subarctic Indians, 136
cave paintings, 5, 98, *98*
Cayuga, 33, 45
cedar uses, 101, 109, 112
census figures (1990), 139-40
ceremonies
   California Indians, 104
   Chumash *toloache*, 98
   Navajo, 90, 91
   Northwest Indians, 111-18,
      116
   powwows, 147
   Pueblo, 86-87, 90
   Subarctic Indians, 127-28
   Sun Dance, *70*
   warrior, 70
   See also initiation
chacmools, 23

Chaco Canyon, 11, *12*
Chacs (Maya god), 23
Changing Woman, 91
Chapin, F. H., 11
charms, Inuit, 129
Cherokee, 51, 54-59, *58*, 61
   Civil War, 62, 63
   first Indian newspaper, 57
   1990 population, 139
   Trail of Tears, 59-60, *60*
   tribal council (1984), 63
   Cherokee Phoenix, 57
Cheyenne, 65, 73-74, 78
Chichén Itzá, 22
Chichimeca, 23, 24
Chickasaw, 51, 56, 60, 63
chickees, 54, *54*
chiefs, 70, 115, 116, 117
children
   California baby baskets, 101
   Kachinvaki initiation, 86-87
   Northwest customs, 109, 115
China, 119, 135
Chinook, 109, 110, 119, 120,
   121
Chinook Jargon, 119, 121
Chipewyan, 125, 126, 136
Chippewa. *See* Ojibwa
Choctaw, 51, 54, 56, 60, 63
cholera, 103
Christianity. *See* Catholicism
Chumash, 98, *98*, 99, 102
chunky (ball game), 55
Cibola, 87
cities. *See* urban centers
citizenship, 146
civilization, definition of, 17
Civil War, 61-63
clan, 35-36
Clark, William, 119-20
Clatsop, 120
clay-walled houses, 9-11
Cliff Dwellers. *See* Anasazi
Cliff Palace, 11
cloth, 41, 42, 64, 100, 119
clothing
   Algonquian, 32
   California Indians, 101
   fur trade, 41
   Inuit, 130
   Northwest Indians, 109, 118
   Seminole patchwork, 64
Clovis culture, 8
clowns (Koshare), 87
Coast Salish, 109, 114, 118

Code Talkers, Navajo, 94-95
codices, 21
Cody, William F., 75-76
coins, 119, 122
Colby, Clara, 79
Colby, Leonard W., 79
Colorado, 10, 11, 71
colors
   Chumash rock art, 98
   vegetable dyes, 93, 101,
   114
Columbia River, 120, 145
Columbus, Christopher, 3, 37,
   134
Comanche, 65, 74-75, 76
cone-shaped housing, 54, 126,
   126
confederacies (Native
   American). *See* Iroquois
   Confederacy; Powhatan
   Confederacy
Confederacy (U.S. South), 61-
   63
Connecticut, 43, 47, 142
contemporary Native
   Americans. *See* Native
   Americans today
coppers, *114*, 115, 116
corn, 8, 14, 17, 18, 31, 36, 51-
   53, 85
Coronado, Francisco, 87
Cortés, Hernando, 26-27
cotton, 8
council house, 55
councils, 70
counting coup, 72
courtyards, 55
cradle board, 115
Cradleboard Teaching Project,
   151
crafts
   Anasazi, 10
   California Indians, 101-2
   contemporary, 140
   Hopewell, 14
   Navajo, 92, 93
   Ojibwa, 33
   Olmec, 18-19, 20
   Pueblo, *91, 92*
   Southeast Indians, 52
   See also art; *specific types*
Crazy Horse, 74
creation stories
   Maya, 21
   Navajo, 6, 90

Creator (Iroquois), 37
Cree, 125, 126, 137
Creek, 51, 55, 56, 59, 60, *61*,
   62, 63
crops. *See* farming; *specific
   crops*
Crow woman warrior, 73
culture
   definition of, 8
   See also tradition preservation
Curtis, Edward, *116*
Custer, George Armstrong, 73

D
Dakota Sioux, 65
Dakota uprising, 72
dances
   Booger Dance, 56
   Ghost Dance, 77-79
   kachina, 86, 87
   powwow competitions, 147
   Sun Dance, 68, *69*, 81
   war, 70
   White Deerskin Dance, 104
   winter ceremonials, *116,*
   117-18
Dances with Wolves (film),
   150
deer, 100, 109, 130
Deer, Ada, 47
dehorning ceremony, 36
De Soto, Hernando, 55
dialects, 99
diet. *See* food
Diné (Navajo), 89
disease decimation
   California Indians, 102-3,
   104, 107
   Inuit, 136
   Northeast Indians, 41
   Northwest Indians, 120
   Pueblo Indians, 88, 93
dogs, 71, *114*, 131, *132*, 133
dolls, kachina, 87
dream-guessing, 38
drop the bomb event, 138
drought, 11-12, 26, 88
drypaintings, 91
dugouts, 30-31
Dutch traders, 41, 42-43
dyes, 93, 101, 113
Dzonkwa, 117-18

E
ear pull event, 138

effigy mounds, 12
elk, 100, 109
El Salvador, 17
embroidery, 136
employment, 140, 141, 151
Enchanted Owl, The (print),
   135
England, 44-45
English colonists, 37-41, 43,
   44-45, 55-56
English traders, 41, 44, 118,
   119, *135*
Erdrich, Louise, 148
Erie, 33, 42
Eskimo. *See* Inuit
Estevan, 87
eulachon fish oil, 112
Evil Twin, 36
Eyre, Chris, *149*

F
False Faces, 36-37
famine, 88, 93
farming
   California Indians, 100
   Mesoamerica, 17-18, 20, 23
   Mississippian, 14
   Northeast Indians, 31, 36-37,
   40
   reservations, 72
   Southeast Indians, 51-52
   Southwest Indians, 8, 9, 83,
   85-86, 88-90
   See also food
fasting, 22, 52, 53
federal recognition, 146
felt hats, 42
festivals. *See* ceremonies
fiberglass boats, 138
films, *149*, 150, 151
First Man, 90
First Salmon Ceremony, 111-12
First Woman, 91
fishing, 30, 53, 99
   Inuit, 129-30
   Northwest Indians, 110-12,
   111, 117, 122-23
Five Civilized Tribes, 56, 61-63
Five Nations. *See* Iroquois
   Confederacy
floral embroidery, 136
Florida, 51, 54-55, 59, 78
Fonseca, Harry, 141
food
   California Indians, 99-100

first Indians, 8
Inuit, 129-30
Lewis and Clark expedition, 122
Northwest Indians, 109-12
Subarctic Indians, 125
See also farming; fishing; hunter-gatherers
Fool Dancers, 118
footrace, 96
Fort Apache Indian Reservation, 140
Fort Clatsop, 120
Fort Laramie, 71
Fort Marion drawings, 78
Fort Michilimackinac, 45
forts, 71
Forty-Niners, 93
Four Corners area, 10
Foxwoods Casino, 142
French and Indian War, 44, 45
French traders, 41, 42, 44, 55, 119, 137, 139
fur trade, 41-43, 118, 135
Maritime, 118-19, 120
Métis, 136-37, 139

G
Gabrielino, 99, 104, 105
gathering. *See* hunter-gatherers
Gathering of Nations, 149
Georgia, 51, 59, 62
Ghost Dance, 77-79, *77*
gift-giving, 43, 115-17, *116*
Gila River Indian Reservation, 140
Glittering World, 6
goggles, *134*
Gold Rush, 93, 105-6
Good Twin, 36
Grand Council of the Iroquois, 34
Grand Medicine Society. *See* Midewiwin
granite, 19
grasshopper, roasted, 100
grass shelters, 101
graves. *See* burial mounds; burial sites
Great Lakes, 29, 30, 32, 45, 46, 48
Great Law, 33
Great Plains, 67 (*see also* Plains Indians)
Great Serpent, 46

Great Serpent Mound, 14
Great Temple of Tenochtitlán, *25*
Green Corn Ceremony, 52-53, 55
Greene, Graham, 149
Greenland, 128, 134, *135*
Green Tea Ceremony, 55
Guatemala, 17, 20, 22
guns, 42, 71, 76, 119, 120, 138
Gwich'in, 125, 126

H
Haida, 109, *113*
hallucination, 98
Hamatsa Dance, *116*, 118
Hamatsa Society, 118
Hano (village), 89
Harjo, Joy, 148
harpoons, 110, 128, 130, 138
Harrison, William Henry, 46, 47
Hayes, Ira, *95*
head-flattening, *115*
head sculpture, *19*
healers
California Indians, 104
Iroquois, 36-37
Nootka, 110
Ojibwa, 32
Hendrick, Chief, 44
herring, 110
Hiawatha, 33-34
Hidatsa, 65
hides, 67, 68, 70, 127, 132
as trade objects, 71, 76
hieroglyphs, 21
Hill, Jack, *48*
Hodenosaunee, 35
hogan, 91-92, 94
Hohokam, 8, 9-10, *9*, 83
Honduras, 17
hooks, 30, 110
Hopewell Culture, 12, 13-14
Hopi, 84, 85, 86, 89
Horn, Peter, *48*
horses, 66, 67, 92
House Made of Dawn (Momaday), 148
housing
California Indians, 100, 101
Hohokam, 9
Inuit, 131-32, 134
Mogollon, 10
Northwest Indians, 109, 112

Plains Indians, 67, 71
Southeast Indians, 54-55, *54*
Southwest Indians, 83, 84-85, 91-92
Subarctic Indians, 126, *126*
See also specific types
Houston, James, 135
hozho (Navajo concept), 91
Huitzilopochtli (god), 24-25, 26
human sacrifice, 18, 22, 23, 26
hunter-gatherers, 71
Algonquian, 31-32
California Indians, 99-100, 101
Mound Builders, 13
Northwest Indians, 109-10, 122
Southeast Indians, 53
hunters, 6, 7
Aleut, 128, 137-38
fur trade, 41, 42, 120
Inuit, 129, 130, 131, 132, 133, *133*, 136
Plains Indians, 65, 66, *66*
Southeast Indians, 53
Subarctic Indians, 125-27, *126*, 137-38
See also buffalo; whale hunting
Hupa, 104
Huron, 33, 34, 38, 42, 46
huskies, 131, *132*
hyacinth plants, 100

I
ice age, 7
Iceland, 132
Idaho, 81
igloos, 131-32, 134
Illinois, 14, 46
income, 141
Indiana, 13, 14, 46
Indian Removal Act of 1830, 58
Indians of All Tribes, 108
Indian Territory, 58-64
Ingalik, 125
initiation, 70, 86, 90, 117
Innu (Montagnai-Naskapi), 125, 128
intermarriage, 137
International Whaling Commission, 123
Internet, 151

InterTribal Bison Cooperative, 82
Inuit, 3, 128-35, *132*, *134*
  contact with non-Indians, 134-36
  current population, 139
  Nunavut territory, 146
  World Eskimo-Indian Olympics, 138, *138*
Iowa, 14
"iron horses," 72
Iroquoian, 29, 32-37
Iroquois Confederacy, 33-37, 42-49, *48*
  American Revolution division, 45
  current status, 146
  reservations, 46-47
  wars, 42-45
irrigation, 85-86
Ishi (last surviving Yahi), 106-7
Itzamna (Maya god), 23
Iwo Jima flag-raising, *95*
Ix Chel (Maya god), 23

J
Jackson, Andrew, 57
jade, 19
jaguar, 19, 23
Jamestown Colony (Va.), 37, 39-40
Japan, 94-95
Jefferson, Thomas, 119
Jesuits, 44
jobs, 140, 141
Johnson, Emily Pauline, 47
Johnston, Philip, 94
Joseph, Chief, *80*, 81
jump-kill (buffalo), 67, 68

K
kachina dolls, 87
kachinas, 86, 87
Kachinvaki, 86-87
Kansas, 14, 46
Kateri Tekakwitha, 44
kayaks, 127, 128
Keepers of the Central Fire, 33-34
Kennewick Man, 145
Kenojuak, 135
Kentucky, 13
King Philip's War, 40-41
Kinich Ahau (Maya god), 23
Kiowa, 59, 65, 78, 148

kiva, 86, 88
knuckle hop event, 138, *138*
Koshare, 87
Kroeber, Alfred, 106-7
Kwakiutl, 109, 115-16, 117, 118

L
La Claire, Joe, *48*
lacrosse, 45, 55
Laguna Pueblo, 89, 148
Lakota Sioux, 65, 71, 73-74, 76, 77-81
  current land claim, 145-46
  tradition preservation, 81
lamps, 130, 134
lance, 70
land claims, 137, 145-46
land losses
  California Indians, 106
  Confederate allies, 63
  Northeast Indians, 46, 48-49
  Northwest Indians, 121-22
  removal policy, 58-61, 63
  termination policy, 49
languages
  California Indians, 99
  Chinook Jargon, 119, 121
  current status, 147
  Nahuatl, 26
  Navajo, 94-95
  Nootka, 115
  sign, 65
La Venta, 18
legends
  Inuit, 130-31
  Iroquois, 36-37
  Navajo, 6, 90, 94
  oral tradition, 5
Lenape, 29, 43
Lewis, Meriwether, 119-20, 122
Lewis and Clark expedition, 119-20, 122
Lincoln, Abraham, 72
Little Bighorn River, 73
Little Big Man (film), 150
Little Crow, 72
Longfellow, Henry Wadsworth, 34
longhouse, 34-35, 36-37
Long Walk, 92-93
Los Angeles (Calif.), 140
Lost Bird, 79-80
Lost Bird Society, 80
Lost Colony, 37-38

Louisiana, 14, 51
Louisiana Purchase, 119-20
Lower Creek, 62
Luiseño, 99, 104
Lumbee, 38, 146

M
Mackinac Island (Mich.), 45
Maine, 47
Makah, 109, 110, 123
Mandan, 65
Manhattan island, 43
Manitoba (Canada), 65, 137
maple syrup, 30
marionettes, 116
Maritime Fur Trade, 118-19
Marquina, Ignacio, *25*
marriage, 35-36
Martinez, Julian, 91
Martinez, Maria, 91
Mashantucket Pequot, 43, 47, 142
masks
  Cherokee, 56
  Iroquois, 36-37
  kachina, 86, 87, 88
  Northwest Indians, 116, *116*, 118
Massachusetts, 30, 37, 40
Massasoit, 40
mathematics, 21
mat houses, 100
Maya, 17, 18, 20-23, 24
McIntosh, William, *61*, 62
Me and Mine (Sekaquaptewa), 85
measles, 41, 103
medicine men. *See* healers
Menominee, 29, 30, 46, 49
Menominee Restoration Act of 1973, 49
Mesa Verde, 11
Mesoamerica, 17-28
Metacom (King Philip), 40-41
Métis, 3, 137, 139
Mexican cession (1848), 89, 105
Mexican War, 105
Mexico, 8, 17-28, 96, 104-5
Mexico City, 19, 24, *25*
mica, 18, 19
Michigan, 14, 43, 45, 46, 48
Micmac, 29
Midewiwin, 32, 49
Mimbres Valley, 9, 10

mineral rights, 137
miniature baskets, 102, *102*
Minnesota, 72
missionaries
  California Indians, 102,
    103-5
  Northeast Indians, 44, 46-47
  Pueblo Indians, 81
  Southwest Indians, 88
  Subarctic Indians, 138
missions, 103-5, *103*
Mississippi, 51, 61
Mississippian Culture, 12, 14,
  15-16
Mississippi River, 14, 16, 58,
  119
Mississippi River Valley, 65
Missouri, 15
Miwok, 99
Mixcoatl, 23
Mogollon, 9, 10, 83
Mohave, 85
Mohawk, 33, 35, 42-43, 44, 45,
  47
  steelworkers, 48, *48*
Momaday, N. Scott, 148, *148*
Monks Mound, 15
Montagnais-Naskapi. *See*
  Innu
Montana, 71, 73-74, 122
Montezuma, 27
moose, 125
Morgan, Thomas J., 82
mother civilization, 18
Mound Builders, 12-16
Mount Lassen, 106
movies, *149,* 150
museums, 142, 145, 149-50

N
Nahuatl language, 26
Nakai, R. Carlos, 149
Nakota, 65
Nanbozho, 34
Nanye'hi (Nancy Ward), 56
Narragansett, 29, 31, 40-41
Natchez, 51
National Committee to Save
  the Menominee People and
  Forest, 47
National Museum of the
  American Indian, 149-50,
  150
Native American Church, 75,
  147-49

Native American Graves
  Protection and Repatriation
  Act of 1990, 145
Native American rights, 82,
  107-8, 143, 144-45, *144,* 151
Native Americans today, 139-
  50
  Cherokee tribal council, 63
  citizenship, 146
  common misconception,
    151
  federal recognition, 146
  largest tribes, 139
  name preference, 3
  Navajo, 95-96
  Northeast communities, 47-
    49, 139
  population, 63-64, 107-8,
    139
  Subarctic and Arctic hunters,
    137-38
Navajo, 83, 84, 89-96
  creation story, 6, 90
  encounters with non-
    Indians, 92, 93
  1990 population, 139
  Pueblo contact, 89-90, 93
Navajo Code Talkers, 94-95
Navajo Indian Reservation, 93,
  95-96, 140
Navajo Nation, 95-96
negative numbers, 21
Neihardt, John C., 81
neophytes, 103
Netherlands. *See* Dutch traders
nets, 30, 110
Neutral, 33, 42
Newfoundland, 37
New Mexico, 9, 10, 12, 83, 87,
  89, 92-93, 95, 105
  current Native American
    population, 140
  powwow, 149
New York City, 140
New York State, 13, 14, 32, 46,
  47-48, 140
Nez Perce, 81
Nicaragua, 17
nightmares, 38
Niro, Shelley, 141
Nisenan, 99
Nixon, Richard M., 47
Niza, Marcos, 87
Nootka, 109, 110, 115, 119
Norsemen, 134

North Carolina, 29, 33, 37, 38,
  51, 146
Northeast Indians, 29-49
  current communities, 47-48,
    139
Northern Paiute, 77
Northwest Indians, 109-23
  Aleut similarities, 128
  California tribes, 99
  contact with non-Indians,
    118-21
  reservations, 121-22
  trading skill, 118
Northwest Passage, 134-35
Not Help Him, Marie, 80
Nova Scotia, 29
Nunavut, 146
nuts, 100, 101

O
Oa trench, 7
Obomoswin, Alanis, 150
obsidian, 18, 19, 20
Ohio, 13, 14, 43, 46
Ohio River Valley, 45
Ohonharoia ceremony, 38
oil
  Alaskan Native rights, 137
  blubber, 130, 134
  eulachon fish, 112
Ojibwa (Chippewa), 29, *31,*
  32, 33, 44, 45, 49
  1990 population, 139
Oklahoma, 47, 58, 59, 63, 64,
  140, 149
Oklahoma City (Okla.), 140,
  149
Olmec, 17, 18-20
Oñate, Juan de, 88
Oneida, 33, 45, 46
Onondaga, 33-34, 35, 45
oral tradition, 5
Oregon, 99, 109, 121
Osceola, 59, 63
Ottawa, 44, 45
Our Mother (Iroquois), 36

P
Pacific Coast, 99, 108, 109,
  110-11, 117, 120
pan-Indianism, 143
Papaga (Tohono O'Oodham),
  10, 83
parkas, 130
Parker, Cynthia, 76

Parker, Quanah, 74-75, 76
Parry, William Edward, *135*
patchwork, 64
Paucatuck, 43
Pawnee, 59, 65, 69
Peacemaker, 33
Peltier, Leonard, 143
Pennsylvania, 13, 14
Penobscot Reservation, 47
Pequot, 43, 47, 142
Pequot War, 43
performers, famous, 149, 151
Petun, 42
peyote, 75, 147-49
Philip of Macedon, 41
Pilgrims, 40
Pima (Akimel O'Oodham), 10, 33, 93
Pine Ridge Indian Reservation (S.D.), 78, 79, 81-82, 140, 143
pit houses, 8, 9, 101
"place of the cactus," 26
Plains Indians, 65-82
    contact with non-Indians, 71
    current Sioux population, 139
    Ghost Dance, 77-79
    groups, 65
    horse's importance, 66, 67
    movie depictions, 150
    warriors, 68-70, 72
    wars with U.S. Army, 69, 73, 74-75, 76, 79-81, 151
    women's roles, 70-71
    See also buffalo
plank boats, 99
plank houses, 101, 109, 112
plants. *See* farming; wild plants
Plymouth Colony (Mass.), 37, 40-41
Pocahontas, 38-40, *39*
polar bear, 133
Pomo, 99, 102, *102*
Pontiac, 45
Pontiac's War, 45
Pope (Pueblo leader), 88
population, current, 47, 63-64, 107-8, 139, 140, 151
Popul Vuh, 21
potatoes, 51
Potawatomi, 29, 44, 45, 46
potlatches, 115-17
pottery
    Catawba, 53

Mogollon, 9, 10
    Pueblo, *91*, 92
poverty, 141-42
Poverty Point, 14, 15
Powhatan, 38-39, 40
Powhatan Confederacy, 29
powwows, 146
prehistoric cultures, 5-9
    California, 97
    Kennewick Man, 145
    Mound Builders, 12-16
Preloch, 76
printmaking, 135
Pueblo Bonito, 11, *12*
Pueblo Indians, 12, 83-90, 99
    contact with Spaniards, 83, 87-89
    farming, 85-86
    Navajo contact, 89-90, 93
    pottery, *91*, 92
    religion, 86-87, 88, 89
    tradition continuance, 89
Pueblo Revolt of 1680, 88
pueblos, 83, *84*
    layout, 84-85
Puget Sound, 109
pumpkin, 51
Pyramid of the Sun, 20
pyramids, 14, 18, 21

Q
quail, 100
Quebec (Canada), 43
Quechan, 85
Quezalcóatl (god), 26, 27

R
rabbits, 100
racherías, 105
railroads, 63, 72
rain making, 86
ranching, 92
Raven, 118
Red Cloud's War, 71
Red Earth Festival, 148-49
Red Power, 143-44
Red River, 137
religion
    artifact repatriation, 145
    Aztec, 24-25, 26, 27, 28
    California Indians, 104
    Catholic missions, 103-5, *103*
    Chumash *toloache* rituals, 98
    Lakota revival, 81

Maya, 22, 23
Mesoamerica, 18, 21, 22, 23, 24, 27, 28
Native American Church, 75, 147-49
Navajo, 91, 92
Northeast Indians, 32, 37, 45-46
Plains Indians, 67, 68, 75, 77-80, 81
Pueblo Indians, 86-87, 88, 89
Subarctic Shaking Tent Ceremony, 127-28
See also Catholicism; missionaries
relocation program, 107
removal policy, 57-61
repatriation, 144-45
reservations
    Comanche, 75
    current status, 141, 142
    Hopi, 89
    Indian coping methods, 77-78
    Navajo, 93, 95-96, 140
    Northeast Indians, 47, 48
    Northwest Indians, 121-22
    Plains Indians, 71, 72, 73, 74, 75, 77-78, 79, 81-82, 140, 143
    termination policy, 49
Return of the Sun (print), 135
Riel, Louis, Jr., 137
rifles, 76, 138
Rio Grande, 12
Rio Grande Pueblo, 89
Rio Grande Valley, 84
Roanoke Colony (N.C.), 37-38
rock paintings, 5, 98, *98*
Rocky Mountains, 65, 119, 122
Rolfe, John, 39
roots, 99, 122
Ross, John, 62, *135*
round houses, 91-92
Rowlandson, Mary, 41
rugs, Navajo, 93, 94
Running Eagle (Brown Weasel Woman), 73
Russian explorers and traders, 118, 119, 127, 136

S
Sacagawea, 122
sacrifice. *See* human sacrifice

St. Augustine (Fla.), 78
Sainte Marie, Buffy, 151
St. Lawrence River, 48
St. Louis (Mo.), 15
Salinan, 99
Salish, 119
salmon, 99, 110, 111-12
San Carlos Mission, 105
San Francisco (Calif.), 48, 107, 108, 140
San Gabriel Mission, 104, 105
San Ildefonso Pueblo, 91
San Lorenzo, 18, *19*, 20
San Luis Rey Mission, 104
Santa Barbara (Calif.), 102
Saskatchewan (Canada), 65
scarecrows, 130
science, Maya, 21
sculpture
    Maya, 22
    Mississippian, 14
    Northwest totem pole, 112-13
    Olmec, 19, *19*, 20
    Toltec, 23
seal hunting, 130, 133
    furs and skins, 119, 120, 130, 132
sea otters, 128
Seattle (Wash.), 109
Seattle, Chief, *123*
Sedna, 130-31
seeds, 99
Sekaquaptewa, Helen, 85
self-determination, 144
Seminole, 54-56, *54*, 59, 60, 61, 62, 63, 64
Seminole Resistance, 59, 62
Seneca, 33, 35, 36, 42-43, 45
Sequoyah, 57, *58*, 63
Seven Cities of Cibola, 87
Seventh Cavalry, 79
Shagodyowehgowah, 37
Shaking Tent Ceremony, 127-28
shamans, 127-28
Shawnee, 45
sheepherding, 92
shellfish, 30, 110
shells, decorated, *9*, 14
Shenandoah, Joanne, 149
shields, 70
Shoshone, 122
Sierra Nevada, 99
sign language, 65

Silko, Leslie Marmon, 148
Sioux, 65, 77-81
    land claim, 145-46
    1990 population, 139
    Pawnee rivalry, 69
    Red Cloud's War, 71
    reservation, 71, 72, 74, 75, 78
    See also Lakota Sioux
Sitting Bull, 74, 76
skyscrapers, 48
slave ownership, 57, 63
Slavey, 125
sleds, dog, 131, *132*, *135*
smallpox, 41, 103, 120
Smith, Jaune Quick-to-See, 141
Smith, John, 39-40
Smithsonian Institution, 149
Smoke Signals (film), 149
Snaketown, 10
snowmobiles, 138
snowshoes, 126
snowsnakes, 36
social ranks
    Aleut, 128
    Mesoamerica, 18
    Northwest Indians, 112-17
societies
    Hamatsa, 117
    Midewiwin, 32, 47
    warrior, 70
Society of American Indians, 143
sod houses, 131-32
song duel, 132-33
"Song of Hiawatha, The" (Longfellow), 34
sorcery conviction, 88
Soto, Hernando de, 55
South Carolina, 33, 51, 55, 61
South Dakota, 77-78, 81-82, 140, 143
    Black Hills, 72-73, 82, 145-46
Southeast Indians, 51-64
    current population, 63-64, 139
Southwest Indians, 83-96
    current population, 139
    major cultures, 8-12
Spanish explorers, 11, 55, 66
    California Indians, 102
    Mesoamerica, 22, 23, 26-27
    Navajo Indians, 92
    Northwest Indians, 118

Pueblo Indians, 83, 87-89
Spanish missions, 103-5, *103*
spears, 30, 110, 130
Spider-woman, 94
spirit world, 113, 116, 117-18, 126-28
sports
    ball courts, 10, 22, 55
    lacrosse, 45, 55
    snowsnakes, 36
    World Eskimo-Indian Olympics, *137*, 138
squash, 8, 14, 36
steel construction workers, 48, *48*
stelae, 21
Stevens, Isaac, 121, 122
strawberries ("heartberries"), 31
Subarctic and Arctic Indians, 125-38
    Arctic groups, 128-35, 137-38
    Subarctic groups, 125-28, 136-38
    Subarctic Métis, 137
Sun Dance, 68, *69*, 81
supernatural, 19, 113, *116*, 117
Sutter's Fort (Calif.), 105
sweat lodge, 67
symbols
    Cherokee, 57, *58*
    Maya, 21
    Navajo, 91

T
Talking God, 92
Tarahumara, 96
Tarbell, John, *48*
tattoo, 85
Tecumseh, 45-46
temples, Aztec, 24-25, 26
Tennessee, 51
Tenochtitlán, 24-25, 26, 27, 28
Tenskwatawa, 45-46
tents, 132
Teotihuacán, 19-20
termination policy, 47
Texas, 65, 105
Thadodaho, 33
Thanksgiving, 40
Three Sisters, 36
Tikal, 21
Tillamook, 117
Timucua, 51, *52*

Tipai, 99
tipi, 67, 71
Tippecanoe, 46, 47
"Tippecanoe and Tyler too,"
   47
Tlatelolco, 25
Tlingit, 109, 119
tobacco, 100
Tohono O'Oodham (Papago),
   10, 83
toloache rituals, 98
Toltec, 17, 23-24, 25
tools
   California Indians, 101
   Inuit, 130
   Northeast Indians, 41
   Northwest Indians, 110, 113
Topiltzin, 23
totem poles, 112-14, *113*
Toypurina's Rebellion, 105
trade
   Arctic Indians, 134-36
   Cahokia, 16
   Chinook as middlemen, 120
   Chinook Jargon, 119, 121
   Hopewell, 14
   Inuit, 133-35
   Mesoamerica, 18
   Northeast Indians, 41-42
   Northwest Indians, 113, 114,
      118-19, 120, 121
   Plains Indians, 71, 72
   sign language, 65
   Subarctic Indians, 136
   See also fur trade
trading posts, 94, 134
tradition preservation, 5, 64,
   149
   Black Elk, 81
   Northeast Indians, 49
   Pueblo, 89
   repatriation, 145-46
   Yahi culture, 107
Trail of Tears, 59-60, *60*, 63
transformation masks, 116
travois, 71
treaties, 47, 58, 63, 146
   Plains Indians, 72, 73
   Washington Indians, 121-23
Treaty of Fort Laramie (1868),
   73
Treaty of Indian Springs
   (1825), 62
Treaty of Point Elliot, *123*
trenches, 7, 8

tribes
   current largest, 139
   federal recognition, 146
   Indian Territory
      dispersal/re-formation,
      63-64
   See also specific tribes
tribute, 25-26
Tsimshian, 117
tuberculosis, 107
Tula, 23
tule (bulrush), 100
Tulsa (Okla.), 140
Tunica, 51, 61
Tuscarora, 33, 45, 46, 51
Tutlthidi, 114
Tyler, John, 47

U
Uayeb, 22
umialik (whale hunter), 130
Unangan. *See* Aleut
University of California, 106-7
Upper Creek, 62
urban centers
   current Native American
      population, 47, 140
   Mesoamerica, 18, 19-20, 21,
      23, 24-25, 26, 27, 28
U.S. Army
   Cherokee removal, 59-60, 61
   Pawnee scouts, 69
   wars with Plains Indians, 71,
      73-75, 76, 78-81, 151
U.S. government, 65, 72, 93,
   95, 107, 121-22
   current policies, 136, 142,
      144-46, 149-50
   removal policy, 57-61
   termination policy, 47
U.S. Marines, 94, 95, 95
Utah, 10

V
vegetable dyes, 93, 101, 113
village councils, 36
villages
   Aleut, 128
   California Indians, 97, 98-99
   Northwest Indians, 109, 128
   Pueblo Indians, 83, 84, 89
   Southeastern Indians, 55
Virginia, 37, 39-40

W
walrus, 130, 132

Wampanoag, 29, 30, 40-41
wampum, 43-44
Wamsutta, 40
war captives, 22, 34, 43, 69
war clubs, 70
war dances, 70
Ward, Brian, 56
Ward, Nancy (Nanye'hi), 56
warlike people
   Iroquois, 34, 43
   Maya, 20-21
   Plains Indians, 68-70
   Toltec, 23
warriors, 69-70
   counting coup, 72
   Crazy Horse, 74
   women, 73
Washington State, 99, 109, 121,
   122, 145
water, Hopi valuation, 85
Watie, Stand, 62
weapons, Plains, 70
weaving
   Hohokam, 9
   Navajo, 92, 93, 94
   See also baskets; blankets
Weetamoo, 40
weirs, 110
were-jaguar, 19
West Virginia, 13
Whale House, 110
whale hunting, 110, 123, 129,
   130, 136, 138
White, John, 37
White Deerskin Dance, 104
white westward migration, 71,
   105, 121
wigwam, 32
wild plants, 99, 100, 101
wild rice, 30, *31*, 49
Wild West Show, 75-76
windigos, 127
Winter ceremonials, *116*, 117-
   18
winter counts (calendars), 69
Wisconsin, 14
Woman Chief of the Crow, 73
women
   Bureau of Indian Affairs
      post, 47
   Catawba potters, 53
   Cherokee Beloved Woman,
      56
   as crop tenders, 51-52
   Inuit activities, 130, 135

Iroquois power, 34, 36, 37
Lewis and Clark expedition
  guide, 122
Navajo activities, 94
Northwest Indian activities,
  111
Plains Indian activities, 70-
  71
warrior, 73
wood carvings, 110, 112-14,
  113, 117, 134
World Eskimo-Indian
  Olympics, 138, *138*

World War II, 94-95, *95*
Wounded Knee Massacre
  (1890), 79-81
Wounded Knee II (1973), 82
Wounded Knee Survivor's
  Association, 80
Wovoka, 77, 78
writers, famous, 148
writing systems
  Cherokee, 57, *58*
  Maya, 21
Wyandot, 43, 46
Wyoming, 72-73

Y
Yahi, 106-7
Yamasee, 51, 55, 59
Yamasee War, 55
Yellow World, 6
Yokut, 99

Z
Zakaeus, Hans, *135*
zero symbol, 21
Zintkala Nuni (Lost Bird), 79-
  80
Zuni, 37, 84

PHOTOGRAPHY CREDITS